11328

9 39598724

POSTWAR
BRITISH
MILITARY
AIRCRAFT

A COLOUR PHOTOGRAPHIC RECORD FROM 1945-1970

TONY BUTTLER

MIDLAND

To my great friend Phil Butler

First published 2012

ISBN 978 1 85780 329 7

Published by Midland Publishing

an imprint of Ian Allan Publishing Ltd, Hersham,
Surrey KT12 4RG.

Printed in China.

Visit the Ian Allan Publishing website at
www.ianallanpublishing.com

Distributed in the United States of America and
Canada by BookMasters Distribution Services.

Contents

FRONT COVER Gloster Javelin FAW.Mk 7 XH756. *See page 114.*

BACK COVER Hunter F.Mk 6s, XE530 'A' and XF417 'B'. *See page 122.*

Introduction

Those of you who either work in aviation or are just enthusiasts and who might be familiar with my publications will know that many of them have specialised in the design and development of military aircraft. However, as a full-time aviation historian one must take whatever work comes along. Fortunately for me that has included a good number of titles in the well-known Warpaint series of books for modellers. When I was about to start my first Warpaint back in the 1990s the founder of that series, the late Alan Hall, told me that he always liked to include some original colour photos of the aircraft type being described in a particular title, assuming that they were available. The subject of that first Warpaint was the Gloster Javelin and a search began for colour shots of this fighter, a move which also started a new hobby for me. Now, besides searching for original documents and project brochures for new aircraft designs and proposals, I began a quest for vintage colour photos of as many British combat and research aircraft as I could find. After fifteen years the result is this book, which I hope will appeal to many aviation enthusiasts and modellers.

The hunt began with the photo files from current and former UK aircraft manufacturers, some of which provided spectacular finds. However, other firms appear to have adopted colour film at a rather late stage, having preferred to stay with black and white. From a modeller's point of view a weakness of manufacturers'

photos is that they often show new aircraft prior to their delivery to an air arm, i.e. without unit markings. Official Ministry colour images can often address that gap, but usually it comes down to the air and ground crew and enthusiasts who took their own images to provide a good selection of 'in service' photos.

The ideal would have been to present a balanced selection of photos for each major type of fighter, bomber and research aircraft, but of course this is impossible. Coverage of any aircraft is limited by what colour is available for that type and also its quality for reproduction. It seems that few postwar military aircraft designs have escaped the colour camera and indeed items are still turning up, but some one-off airframes never survived long enough to have any colour pictures taken of them - indeed certain aircraft like the Handley Page HP.88 were recorded by only a small number of black and white images. One of my favourite aeroplanes is the Armstrong Whitworth AW.52 jet-powered flying wing research aircraft and colour cine film of this machine does exist, but no good quality

ABOVE Photographed on 5 June 1970 and so just falling within the time period covered here, de Havilland Sea Vixen FAW.Mk 1 XJ488 is pictured while serving with the Royal Navy Test Squadron at A&AEE, Boscombe Down, for which it was specially painted in this black and white colour scheme. *Adrian Balch*

colour photos have been traced. However, some contributors were in the lucky position of being able to record rare subjects like the 1950s and 1960s one-off research aircraft.

Moving on to types that were built in quantity, there would often be one-off examples of these modified or repainted for a specific task. The colour camera captured some of them but others have sadly escaped – unless any reader knows better of course! Indeed, if anyone has further vintage colour views from the 1945 to 1970 period which he or she feels are of publishing standard do please contact the publisher or the author. You never know, we might even manage a Volume 2 one day. Just to round off this discussion, a few black and white images of some one-off jet-powered types have been included here to complete the coverage.

For aircraft types flying around the end of the war and into the mid to late 1940s the majority of photos come from official photographers and the press, and for this book we have been given permission to use colour images from the archive of the famous magazine *The Aeroplane*, which today resides in the hands of the historical and preservation magazine of the same name. Few amateur British photographers would have had access to colour in the 1940s but their numbers began to grow during the 1950s, to the point where it is possible to provide a full mixture of amateur and professional work. There are, as one might expect, a lot of pictures from the various Farnborough Air Shows since this was one of the few aviation events where until 1956 the public could take a camera. Some of the book's photographs have been published before but in such cases I feel that the examples reproduced again are of such quality or so rare that they demand inclusion.

The book starts with a quick review of the history of colour photographic film before taking a look at individual aircraft types under an A-Z of their manufacturers. The A-Z is far from being a complete list for the British aircraft industry, in part because not every company of course was building frontline military aircraft or research types, but for new readers it does present a basic reference to the postwar industry. The final chapters move on to feature air shows, government establishments, the aviation press and finally pictures taken while aircraft were in service. Although the book officially ends at 1970, the great majority of the images in here date from before about 1965/66, prior to the arrival in British service of

'modern' types like the Hawker Siddeley Harrier and the American McDonnell F-4K Phantom. A few export aeroplanes are included.

Back in the 1950s aviation was an immensely popular subject, not just for enthusiasts but for the public in general. Mainstream newspapers would include plenty of news on all aspects of aviation and they would provide big features for forthcoming air shows. It is hard to believe now but some of the company test pilots were as famous as today's top sportsmen and women and huge crowds attended Farnborough. Much of this enthusiasm came from the tremendous contribution made by aviation in winning the Second World War. In addition, for most of the population the 1950s was a decade of austerity as the country shook off the effects of conflict and rationing, and so aviation and aircraft brought a bit of glamour into the lives of many. During the following decade this began to change as the 'Swinging Sixties' saw the next generations move on to other interests. Sadly, today's consumer and man in the street usually look upon aviation, and perhaps science in the UK in general, as dull subjects but for those still involved, aviation is still a world that can provide excitement and motivation.

To make this book possible I have been in touch with a great number of people in search of colour slides and transparencies, both in industry, museum and private collections. Their help has been enormous and I hope that readers will find at least a few subjects that will bring them much enjoyment. For me it has been a huge pleasure and a great privilege to have the opportunity to work with this material. I am sure that when these folk took their pictures they could never have imagined what a superb record they were securing for the British military aircraft scene in the decades following the Second World War. We cannot thank you enough. I hope this book will serve as a tribute to the photographers, professional and amateur, who took these images, to the many aircraft manufacturing companies who are featured and to the British Aircraft Industry as a whole. Putting it all together has been a joy! For those who were there, or would like to have been there, the album will hopefully provide a window into a world where much has changed and where many elements are now long gone.

Tony Buttler
Bretforton

Acknowledgements

A big thank you must go to the following for their help with this book, in particular for making their precious and unique colour images available to me. I hope I have not left anyone out.

Adrian Balch; Peter Berry; Chris Chatfield and Peter Dance of Air-Britain; Joe Cherrie; Don Clayton; Alan Curry; Richard Curtis; Lt. Cdr. David Eagles; Flt. Lt. John Farley; Lt. Richard Gravestock; Peter Green; David Hedge; Mike Hooks; Graham Hopkin; George Jenks and the team at Avro Heritage; Tim Kershaw and the Jet Age Museum; Lt. Tony Kilner; Roger Lindsay; Wg. Cdr. John Merry; the late Eric Morgan; Maurice Rowe; North West Heritage Group and the late Bob Fairclough; Terry Panopalis; Wg. Cdr. Clive Rustin; the late Mike Stroud; the late Ray Sturtivant; Sir Mark Thomson; Sqn. Ldr. Andy Whitson; Ray Williams.

Uncredited pictures are generally from the author's collection, with the identity of the individual photographers either lost or unknown. If any reader recognises a photo which he has taken, the author apologises for using it without permission.

There are certain individuals who require special thanks.

First, Mike Oakey and Nick Stroud of *Aeroplane* who allowed the author to peruse and use the wonderful collection of colour material held in their magazine's photo archive.

To everyone at Ian Allan for their help, especially Nick Grant and Jay Slater, and indeed for giving me the chance to put this book together - it has been something of a pet subject for so long.

Finally, I must highlight the wonderful assistance I have received yet again from Phil Butler, who has an incredible ability to recognise a venue and work out the date for the most obscure of pictures. Some of the captions in this work would have been pretty bare without Phil's efforts, but then I have appreciated his help over many years on many books and articles.

Thanks Phil!

Aeroplane magazine is still one of the leading publications for aviation history and features a great number of original articles. It is now owned by the Kelsey Publishing Group and Jarrod Cotter is the editor.

Glossary

A&AEE	Aeroplane and Armament Experimental Establishment, Boscombe Down.
AAM	Air-to-air missile.
AI	Air interception.
anhedral	Downward slope of wing from root to tip.
AS	Armstrong Siddeley.
A/S	Anti-submarine.
ASM	Air-to-surface missile.
AWA	Armstrong Whitworth Aircraft Ltd.
BAC	British Aircraft Corporation.
BP	Boulton Paul Aircraft.
CFE	Central Fighter Establishment.
DH	de Havilland.
dihedral	Upward slope of wing from root to tip.
EE	English Electric.
ETPS	Empire Test Pilots' School.
FAA	Fleet Air Arm.
HAL	Hawker Aircraft Limited.
HP	Handley Page.
HSG	Hawker Siddeley Group.
MAEE	Marine Aircraft Experimental Establishment.
NATO	North Atlantic Treaty Organization.
OCU	Operational Conversion Unit.
OTU	Operational Training Unit.
PR	Photo Reconnaissance.
R & D	Research and Development.
RAAF	Royal Australian Air Force.
RAE	Royal Aircraft Establishment, Farnborough.
RAN	Royal Australian Navy.
RN	Royal Navy.
RNAS	Royal Naval Air Station.
RR	Rolls-Royce.
RRE	Royal Radar Establishment.
SBAC	Society of British Aircraft Constructors (now Society of British Aerospace Companies).
TRE	Telecommunications Research Establishment, Malvern.

Chapter One
Colour Photography – A Brief History

In today's world of digital photography new pictures can be made with the minimum of effort and downloaded onto computers for viewing almost instantly. These images can be cleaned up or corrected with special computer programs and one wonders how hard it must be sometimes for younger people who have grown up in the digital age to realise that not too long ago the process of taking pictures was a bit more difficult. Exposing and developing rolls of colour film into individual prints was still the most common form of photography at the start of this new century, and during the 1990s we had experienced the mass production and printing of colour films for the general public. However, when the author was growing up in the 1960s the use of colour for snapshots was still a relatively new hobby for many, and black and white was very common. Twenty years before that, colour film in the UK was a very new medium indeed, even for professionals. From an aviation point of view, black and white dominated until well after the Second World War had ended, but by 1945 high quality colour film had appeared in the form of Kodachrome, a product from the United States.

ABOVE For many years black and white dominated the field of aviation photography and colour only really made its appearance during the Second World War. Monochrome has its advantages in effect and atmosphere but colour provides so much more in the way of information and accuracy. Arguments still rage, for example, about the colour markings used by aircraft flown during the First World War. This view shows two English Electric Lightnings from No. 111 Squadron with the unit's spectacular paint scheme. Left is F.Mk 3 XR714 with the larger fin and right F.Mk 1A XM190. The photo dates from 1965 and marked the replacement of the F.1A by the F.3. *MoD*

The word photography was coined by Sir John Herschel in 1839 and was derived from the Greek words 'photos' (for light) and 'graphos' (write). Colour photography is a format which reproduces natural colours in an image by chemical methods during the photographic processing phase; in contrast, black and white photography uses a media which can reveal shades of grey only, so inventing a true colour film was always going to be the more difficult task. The first black and white photograph to be made using a negative was produced in 1835 by Henry Fox Talbot and the first known permanent colour photograph was created in 1861 by James Clerk Maxwell, a Scottish inventor and mathematician. One medium for making quality colour photographs for the public which did prove successful was the Dufay process. Dufaycolor was based on a four-colour screen photographic process invented in 1908 by Louis Dufay of France and this was introduced as cine film in 1932 and roll film for stills photography in 1935. It proved popular with amateur and professional photographers alike before disappearing in the 1950s.

However, also in 1935 the Eastman Kodak Company in America introduced the first modern 16mm motion picture colour film which it named Kodachrome, and a year later the company produced the first 35mm Kodachrome stills film. For many years this colour reversal film was used by professionals because of its colour accuracy, particularly for images which were to be published in print media, but it was difficult to process, especially for amateurs. With the growing use of digital photography, sales of this film have steadily declined and in June 2009 Eastman Kodak announced that it was to bring the production of Kodachrome to an end. In 1940 Kodak also introduced the Ektachrome series of transparency, stills and cine films, the processing of which was rather easier than Kodachrome. That meant both professionals and amateurs could now process their own exposures. Sadly, towards the end of 2009 it was announced that the production of Ektachrome would also cease. The European rival to the Kodak 'chrome' range was Agfacolor-Neu, which was a slide transparency film first produced by the Agfa Company of Germany in 1936. Ilford, Fuji and other manufacturers have also produced slide film.

Moving on to colour print film for the general public, one of the most important was Kodacolor,

ABOVE One of the earliest forms of colour film available for aviation photography was Dufaycolor, which could provide a rather grainy print. This Dufay picture shows the red private venture Gloster Meteor two-seat trainer demonstrator aircraft G-AKPK at the SBAC Show at Farnborough in 1948. *Peter Berry*

RIGHT The introduction of Kodachrome provided the opportunity for making colour pictures of much higher quality. This posed image of a Vickers Wellington and its crew preparing for another mission was made on a 5in x 4in (12.7cm x 10.2cm) transparency, and was almost certainly taken during the war. *Hugh Cowin*

ABOVE By the early
1940s most British
manufacturers were using
Kodachrome for some of
their publicity photos.
As a result precious
images were made to
record types like this
de Havilland Sea Hornet
fighter TT202 pictured
over the south coast of
England in either June
or July 1947. *BAE Systems
Heritage, Farnborough*

another Eastman Kodak product which in fact was
one of the world's first true colour negative films. This
first appeared in 1942 and from 1958 became
available in 35mm format, but by 2007 the name was
no longer used by Kodak. Almost all of the pictures in
this book come either from original colour slides and
transparencies or from photo prints, a great number
of which are Kodachrome and Ektachrome originals.
A few are Dufay images but this system did not use a
negative for still photos, just a positive.

From a British point of view, during the 1940s and
1950s the leading light in taking pictures of aircraft
in colour was the famous freelance photographer
Charles E. Brown, who first received stocks of
Kodachrome from America in the middle of the war.
These were supplied to allow Brown to photograph
British aircraft for an American magazine and by the
end of the conflict he was using 5in by 4in (12.7 by
10.2cm) sheet transparency and 35mm colour film
along with his black and white stock. The quality of
his colour photography can be seen in the marvellous
Camera above the Clouds series of books published
by Airlife in the 1980s and early 1990s. Also, by the
end of the war, press photographers working for the
British aviation magazines *Flight* and *The Aeroplane*
had got their hands on colour transparency film and
produced what today are rare images, but at the
time the high cost of reproducing colour in print
meant that until the 1950s at least few of their
pictures were ever published.

The taking of colour photos of aircraft by the
general public, or even by members of the armed
forces, was another matter. Slide film for public
consumption became available in around the early
1950s but it was very expensive. The author has
been told that in about 1952 the processing of a
35mm slide film (which then would have been just
twelve exposures only rather than the 24 or 36 we
know today) would cost in current money the
equivalent of over £30 (nearly $50). In addition, the

RIGHT De Havilland
appears to have taken
colour film in its stride.
This close-up of DH.112
Venom NF.Mk 3 night
fighter WX787 taken
in the 1950s provides
marvellous detail for a
modeller. *BAE Systems
Heritage, Farnborough*

use of privately owned cameras on military installations was prohibited, as indeed was the bringing of cameras by the public into open days and air shows at British air bases; however in July 1956 that ban was lifted by the Air Council. Before that date the one exception to the rule was the annual SBAC Air Show at Farnborough where photographic opportunities were available, but then camera ownership in the UK during the 1950s was minimal anyway. Fortunately, some people did own one and that has helped swell the supply of images made available to the author.

If you were lucky enough to have a camera there was still another problem to deal with – the speed of the film itself. This was a measure of a film's sensitivity to light which over the years has been measured on various numerical scales. For the period we are interested in such measurements were given an ASA (American Standards Association) rating and today you can still buy films of 100, 200 or 400ASA speeds. But during the early 1950s the first Kodachrome I colour film available to the public had an ASA speed of just 8, i.e. *very* slow, which caused problems of blur due to camera shake or subject movement. To permit relatively short exposure times bright conditions were a must, and to minimise the risk of blur with long exposure times the camera had to be held steady and the subject had to be moving as little as possible; not so good when trying to photograph an aircraft performing a

display. Keeping the subject sharp was made a little easier with the arrival of Kodachrome II in 1961 which had a speed of 25ASA. One of the benefits of today's computers, however, is that relatively poor quality original images can now have their colours enhanced and corrected, with scratches and marks removed, prior to being published.

So there we have it – the history of colour film and the problems associated with its use during the period covered by this volume. Today we are so used to seeing colour that one can forget just how rare some of the images reproduced in this book really are, but all of them bring life to an era in aviation that stands out as one of the most fascinating. It saw the end of the piston era for combat aircraft and brought the full and complete introduction of jet-powered types. To go with them came advanced wing shapes and guided weapons so, from a technical point of view, the two decades following the end of the Second World War are full of interest. In addition, the advent of the Cold War meant that during the 1950s British air arms were re-equipped with new aircraft in an attempt to match the build-up by the Communist Warsaw Pact. There were lots of squadrons and for a time these were given a relatively free rein in the colours and markings with which they were permitted to adorn their aircraft. Finally, until the merging of the various companies into the British Aircraft Corporation and Hawker Siddeley Aviation in 1960, there were plenty of firms still producing plenty of different aircraft designs to photograph. In many respects this period was the heyday of the British Aircraft Industry and it is time to take a look at some of those aeroplanes.

ABOVE Before the end of the war the British aviation press, particularly in the form of *Flight* and *The Aeroplane*, were taking their first colour photographs. This lovely image presents the third Avro Shackleton maritime patrol aircraft prototype VW135 and comes from the archive of *The Aeroplane*. *Aeroplane*

LEFT Gloster Aircraft, in the form of photographer Russell Adams, also made liberal use of colour film from the early 1950s. Here we see Gloster Meteor T.Mk 7s of the Central Flying School, Little Rissington, in 1953 and recorded by Adams in a climb, a style of picture often practised by this master of his craft. *Jet Age Museum*

RIGHT Official photographers, working for the RAF, the Royal Navy and the various ministries which have governed British military aviation, have been fortunate to get close-ups and visit venues and positions denied to most amateurs and enthusiasts. This scramble by Avro Vulcan V-Bombers was recorded for posterity by a cameraman standing next to the runway at Waddington. *MoD*

ABOVE By the 1950s colour slide film was becoming available to the public, but it was expensive. Short Sperrin bomber prototype VX161 generates a great deal of interest at the 1955 SBAC Farnborough Air Show.

LEFT Most enthusiasts were limited to photographing aircraft on the ground, but that did not stop them from taking pictures of rare subjects or versions of types which were not built in large numbers. Supermarine Scimitar XD277 '101/R' of No. 800 Squadron was photographed at Cottesmore in 1959. *Graham Hopkin*

ABOVE AND LEFT Two of the author's favourite aircraft are the Hawker Hunter and English Electric Lightning fighters. XG164 was built as a Hunter F. Mk 6 and later converted by Armstrong Whitworth to FGA.Mk 9 standard. This shot was made when the aircraft was serving as 'H' with 74 Squadron - it has an 'H' painted beneath the nose. XR768 was the first full production standard Lightning F.Mk 6 to leave the BAC manufacturing line and is seen as 'A', again of No. 74 Squadron, in the late 1960s. Note the overwing tanks. *MoD*

LEFT Hawker Hunter F.Mk 5 WP120 pictured at Mildenhall in 1956 as 'S' of No. 56 Squadron. The 'redness' of this image was a problem often experienced in those days with the quality of the film and its processing. Fortunately, modern computers can restore such images to more natural colours.
Peter Green

FACING PAGE TOP The enthusiast community did not just embrace members of the general public. Fortunately, aircraft and ground crew serving with the RAF and FAA have done their bit to record the aviation scene. This terrific view of de Havilland Sea Vixen XN707 '242' of No. 890 Squadron was taken in 1963/64 by another squadron pilot.
Sir Mark Thomson

FACING PAGE BOTTOM An important picture made by an amateur RAF photographer. It shows a very busy RAF Germany scene in 1961/62 with Hawker Hunter XG127 taxiing past Gloster Javelin XH912 'S' of No. 33 Squadron and towards a Lightning from No. 56 Squadron. This Hunter FR.Mk 10 was serving as 'Y' of No. 2 Squadron.

ABOVE AND RIGHT Colour photography isn't just a case of taking pictures of individual aircraft; it also enables a record of specific types to be built up. For example, two schemes used by Vickers Valiant bombers are shown by images of XD816 and WZ367.

Chapter Two
British Aircraft Companies – A to D

It is not the object of this book to put together an exhaustive record of the companies which formed the British Aircraft Industry, nor indeed to give a full list of the fighter and bomber types that each firm has built. However, the author is aware that there are new readers who will not be familiar with the nature and organisation of the industry, particularly since 2010 marked the fiftieth anniversary for when most of the 'famous names' disappeared into the British Aircraft Corporation and Hawker Siddeley. Memories of those events (the mergers were controversial) fade with the passing of time as we sadly lose many of the people who were there, and so it seems quite sensible to provide some background information to the companies and aircraft represented in these pages. The list is not complete because of course some manufacturers specialised in the civil market or in light aviation and never became involved in major military aircraft programmes, and (as noted in the Introduction) some postwar aircraft types managed to escape the colour camera altogether.

This first batch covers perhaps the most famous British bomber aircraft company (Avro), a naval aircraft specialist (Blackburn), and two most versatile manufacturers who were responsible for producing a great variety of aircraft types (Bristol and de Havilland).

ABOVE VF345 was an early production de Havilland Vampire F.Mk 3 fighter and was built by English Electric. De Havilland used this airframe as a demonstration aircraft. *Aeroplane*

Armstrong Whitworth

Armstrong Whitworth Aircraft (AWA) built up its aircraft manufacturing facilities during the First World War as part of a large engineering and shipbuilding organisation. With factories at Whitley and Baginton and later Bitteswell, AWA was a founder member of the Hawker Siddeley Aircraft Co Ltd when it was created in 1935, and in the 1960 mergers it formed part of the new Hawker Siddeley Group. After the Second World War AWA concentrated on the manufacture of aircraft designed and developed by other companies. The fighter types in question were the Gloster Meteor and Javelin and the Hawker Sea Hawk and Hunter (both of these firms were also members of the Hawker Siddeley organisation). AWA became more involved with the two-seat Meteor night fighter variants after it was given the development programme for this type, Gloster's commitments to build the single-seat marks of the aircraft having left the parent company no time to work on the latest versions. AWA's only all-new research type to fly was the AW.52 flying wing, but during the postwar decades the firm did build the Apollo airliner and the Argosy freight transport, the latter of which was produced in numbers. Colour coverage of the Javelin, Sea Hawk and Hunter comes under their respective designers. Bitteswell was closed in 1983 but Baginton still operates today as a civilian airport.

Armstrong Whitworth AW.52G glider and AW.52

The beautiful flying wing AW.52 made its debut when the first of two examples took off from the Aeroplane and Armament Experimental Establishment (A&AEE) at Boscombe Down for the first time on 13 November 1947. It was constructed at Baginton as a possible test

aircraft for future flying wing airliners and the second machine flew with the Royal Aircraft Establishment (RAE) Farnborough until 1953. This similar scale model test aircraft was built in wood and first taken into the air from Baginton on 2 March 1945, and it was used for drag trials and some lateral and directional control tests well into the 1950s. No suitable colour photos have been traced of the all-white painted AW.52 but an image does exist of the AW.52G glider. Although the AW.52 did attend an SBAC Show (in 1948) for some reason none of the official photographers appear to have taken it in colour, or if they did then the photos are now lost.

ABOVE Unfortunately the author failed to find a quality colour photograph of the full-size Armstrong Whitworth AW.52 research aircraft. This black and white picture consequently fills a gap in the coverage and shows the first example, serial TS363. *Ray Williams*

BELOW The Armstrong Whitworth AW.52G flying wing glider was flown for the first time in 1945. It is seen here at the RAE Golden Jubilee event held at Farnborough on 7 to 9 July 1955. *Peter Berry*

ABOVE LEFT AND RIGHT The first mark of Armstrong Whitworth night fighter was the NF.Mk 11 and these Russell Adams images show WD597 in April 1951, an early production example which went on to join No. 29 Squadron and was scrapped in 1958. A feature of the NF.11 was the heavily framed canopy. *Jet Age Museum*

Armstrong Whitworth Meteor Night Fighter

The requirement for a night fighter version of the Meteor based on the Mk 7 (the two-seat trainer variant of Gloster's day fighter) was identified through the need to fill a gap in Britain's air defences prior to the arrival of the Gloster Javelin all-weather fighter. The Meteor night fighter was thus an interim aircraft to replace the piston-powered wartime de Havilland Mosquito which, by the late 1940s, did not possess sufficient performance to handle potential new jet bomber types. The big difference from earlier Meteors was a longer nose to house a radar scanner. The first night fighter mark was the NF.Mk 11 and the prototype VW413 (a converted T.Mk 7) made its maiden flight on 28 January 1949. The 11 was followed by the NF.Mks 12 and 13, but the ultimate Meteor night fighter was the NF.Mk 14 first flown in October 1953 which featured a new clear-vision sliding canopy and an even longer nose. AWA's involvement with the Meteor development programme in fact continued beyond the Mk 14 because in 1956 the Mk 11 was turned into a target tug for service with the Royal Navy. This version was called the TT.Mk. 20 and a 'prototype' first flew in December 1956. Good colour coverage is available for certain marks of night fighter Meteors and the target tugs.

ABOVE The final Meteor night fighter was the NF.Mk 14 which, for recognition purposes, had a clear-vision sliding canopy for the crew. This picture of WS744 stresses the aircraft's large nose radome; note also the underwing fuel tanks. *MoD*

BELOW Meteor NF.14 WS838 was one of the last batch of night fighters and, after serving with No. 64 Squadron, it joined the Royal Radar Establishment (RRE) at Pershore. Later WS838 went to RAE Bedford where it was painted in this distinct high visibility yellow colour scheme with a black nose. The picture was taken in 1968 and today this airframe is preserved at Baginton.

BELOW Picture of an NF.14 taken at Benson in 1959. The aircraft appears to be one of the WS75x serials. *Peter Green*

Avro

A. V. Roe & Co, named after Alliott Verdon Roe, was formed in 1910 and by the time it became another founder member of Hawker Siddeley in 1935 it had a new factory up and running at Woodford. Another factory was built in 1938/39 at Chadderton in readiness for wartime production (both facilities were close to Manchester) and the Manchester bomber first flown in July 1939 opened a long series of piston bomber programmes for the company. However, besides its heavy bombers and their developments, Avro also flew the Tudor airliner in June 1945 before moving on to its superb delta wing Vulcan jet bomber. Avro's photographic archive was destroyed in the late 1950s in a building fire. The collection almost certainly included colour images of the 707 research aircraft taken by Russell Adams, the photographer who worked for Gloster Aircraft, so manufacturer's colour views of its immediate postwar aircraft are rare. The Woodford factory is due to close in 2012 and manufacturing has ceased at Chadderton, but the latter site still provides in-service support for some current large Royal Air Force aircraft.

Avro Lancaster

The Lancaster bomber was famously produced as a four-engine development of the firm's twin-engined Manchester and made its first flight on 9 January 1941. Of course this aircraft will always be most remembered for its phenomenal Second World War career, but it should not be forgotten that a good number of examples continued to serve the RAF and other air arms deep into the 1950s. The type's early postwar RAF role extended its service as a bomber where

BELOW Avro Lincoln B.Mk.II SX946, with defensive guns removed, pictured on display at West Malling on 3 October 1959 while serving with the RAF Flying College at Manby. *Mike Hooks*

it was soon joined by a follow-on design called the Lincoln (below), but by the 1950s the Lancaster was being used primarily for air/sea rescue and maritime reconnaissance training flying. The type was finally retired in 1956. A fully civilianised transport for service postwar was called the Lancastrian.

Avro Lincoln

Originally known as the Lancaster B.Mk IV and Mk V, the Lincoln was essentially an enlarged, upgraded and more capable Lancaster powered by Rolls-Royce Griffon engines instead of the earlier type's Merlins. The prototype first became airborne on 9 June 1944 and the new bomber went on to equip 29 RAF squadrons and also the air forces of Argentina and Australia. The last RAF Bomber Command unit to fly Lincolns was the Bomber Command Bombing School which retained the aircraft until October 1960, but the Central Signals Establishment kept its Lincolns in the air until 1963. Numerous examples of both Lancaster and Lincoln (and Lancastrian) were also employed as test beds for a large variety of jet and turboprop engines, their underwing engine nacelles proving ideal for the installation of alternative power units.

ABOVE Another view from the July 1955 RAE Golden Jubilee event. Here white-painted Avro Lancaster B.Mk 7 RT690 and a Bristol Beaufighter line up on the Farnborough runway ready for take-off. RT690 was used by Avro and, as shown here, was fitted with a conical nose. *Peter Berry*

BELOW A picture of Avro Lincoln B.Mk II RF570 taken in around 1960 when it was flying with the Bomber Command Bombing School at Lindholme. *Avro Heritage*

Avro York

Although this book is primarily concerned with frontline combat types, the opportunity has been taken to include one or two transport developments and variants of these aircraft, if a quality colour photo is available. An example was the wartime York development of the Lancaster which first flew on 5 July 1942 and featured the Lancaster's wings and tail coupled with a new fuselage and a third (central) fin. They were operated by civilian airlines and RAF Transport Command and a few examples were still flying in the 1960s.

Avro Shackleton

The last programme in the development line leading from the Manchester and Lancaster, the Shackleton dealt with a need for long-range ocean patrol and air/sea rescue and a requirement to replace serving types which had been built during the war. Many features from the Lincoln and the company's Tudor airliner were carried through to the new aircraft but its fuselage was new. The prototype first flew on 9 March 1949 and, in all, 191 examples were manufactured in three different versions, including the MR.Mk 3 which introduced a different wing shape, tip tanks and other changes. The Shackleton stayed in service with the RAF into the early 1990s.

Avro 698 and Vulcan

Avro stayed in the heavy bomber business with its Vulcan medium V-Bomber but this jet aircraft was a very different aeroplane to the piston types that had preceded it, having been designed to deliver nuclear weapons from very high altitudes at targets far away from home base. The Vulcan introduced the triangular-shaped delta wing and the first Type 698 prototype with its pure delta flew on 30 August 1952, before the type had been christened Vulcan. Two versions powered by the Bristol Olympus turbojet served with the RAF and a larger wing was introduced which featured a modified leading edge. The Vulcan served as part of Britain's nuclear deterrent until 1968 and then as a conventional bomber into the 1980s, making

TOP Avro York MW113 went on to join the British Overseas Airways Corporation as G-AGJC *Malmesbury.* *Aeroplane*

CENTRE Avro Vulcan prototype VX770 poses over a glorious cloudscape above southern England, probably as part of the publicity and build-up for one of the mid-1950s Farnborough Shows. *Aeroplane*

BOTTOM A production Avro Vulcan, sadly unidentified, provides close-up detail for the type's forward fuselage, wing and undercarriage and the V-Bomber's famous white colour scheme. The picture was made at Cottesmore in 1959. *Graham Hopkin*

a famous contribution to the 1982 Falklands conflict just before its retirement. Some airframes were converted to in-flight refuelling tankers which stretched the Vulcan's career on to 1984. The Vulcan has always been a favourite aeroplane both with its aircrew and the public.

Avro 707

One problem with the selection of a delta for the Vulcan bomber, a very advanced wing shape for 1947 when the programme was opened, was that in many respects it was an unknown quantity. Quite sensibly a scale model aircraft was ordered from Avro to assess the delta's aerodynamics and the first of what became the Type 707 family of aeroplanes made its maiden flight on 4 September 1949. A series of memorable displays and flypasts were performed by the 707s and the 698 prototypes at SBAC Farnborough Shows during the 1950s and some examples of the scale model went on to complete long careers in research flying. The 707s are also remembered for their very bright paint schemes.

ABOVE In-service pictures of any of the Avro 707 family of research aircraft taken in colour are rare, in part because the Avro photo archive was destroyed in a fire in the late 1950s. It is known that Gloster photographer Russell Adams took shots of one aircraft, but his images must have been lost in the conflagration. This picture is cheating a bit because it shows 707A WZ736 after preservation, but it was taken in 1969 – just in time! During its flying career this aircraft was actually painted orange. *Graham Hopkin*

Blackburn

Blackburn Aircraft Ltd was formed in 1914 but the man after whom it was named, Robert Blackburn, had already been building aircraft for some five years. By 1945 a factory at Brough had become the company's main facility, at which time it was still grappling with the problems of its Firebrand heavy torpedo fighter, the programme for this aircraft having been ongoing through most of the war. The Firebrand did see some service postwar but its successor, the 'Firecrest', did not enter production. General Aircraft was bought by Blackburn in 1949 in a move which strengthened the latter's fortunes in the form of production orders for General's Universal freighter, which entered service as the Beverley. Blackburn then really hit the mark with its splendid Buccaneer naval strike aircraft before becoming another company to form part of Hawker Siddeley in 1960. The Brough factory is still operating today (2012).

Blackburn Firebrand

The design of the Blackburn Firebrand went right back to the early years of the war and the first example began flight testing on 27 February 1942. By the end of hostilities the original Napier Sabre engine had been replaced by a Bristol Centaurus (the new version flew on 21 December 1943) and it was 1945 when examples began to join Fleet Air Arm units for the first time. The Firebrand served with the Navy until 1953 when its strike role was filled by the Westland Wyvern.

Blackburn 'Firecrest'

Three prototypes of this follow-on torpedo fighter to the Firebrand were ordered, powered by a Bristol Centaurus engine. However, the end of the war took away some of the need to get the aircraft ready and so the first example did not fly until 1 April 1947. The flight programme certainly continued into 1949 but there were no production orders. No colour images for this

impressive aeroplane, or indeed for the Firebrand, are available to the author, but Charles Brown did take some excellent images of the Firebrand.

Blackburn Anti-Submarine Aircraft

Three prototype aircraft were ordered as a rival project to the design that became the Fairey Gannet (Chapter Three). The first two were fitted with Rolls-Royce Griffon piston engines as the Blackburn Y.A.7 and Y.A.8 respectively, the first flight taking place on 20 September 1949, but the third aircraft flew on 19 July 1950 with an Armstrong Siddeley Double Mamba turboprop installed. As such this machine was given the SBAC designation Y.B.1, but no colour views have been found for any of these aircraft.

Blackburn Buccaneer

Blackburn's struggles to get the Firebrand ready made a marked contrast to its very successful programme with the Buccaneer. This high performance jet-powered

naval strike aircraft made its first flight on 30 April 1958 and so impressive was the aeroplane that it went on to join the RAF as well. The Navy kept its Buccaneers until the last of its big aircraft carriers (the *Ark Royal*) was retired in 1978, but RAF machines continued flying right through to March 1994 when 208 Squadron was disbanded. The only real weakness experienced by the Buccaneer was the de Havilland Gyron Junior turbojet which powered the forty S.Mk 1 aircraft to be built. This engine did not provide sufficient thrust, especially in hot conditions, which operationally made these aeroplanes inadequate. Consequently, the S.Mk 2 was introduced with the more powerful and much better Rolls-Royce RB.168 Spey turbofan, the first example flying on 17 May 1963. By mid-1968 the Buccaneer S.Mk 2 had fully replaced the S.Mk 1 in the front line, which means unfortunately that the newer aircraft just about falls outside the book's parameters. Buccaneers also served with the South African Air Force.

ABOVE LEFT XK489 was the first fully navalised Buccaneer and is shown in Malta in about 1960 during the aircraft's trials programme. *AE Hughes via the late Ray Sturtivant*

ABOVE RIGHT Another Buccaneer development aircraft was XK527 which is seen here in Malta undergoing preparations for a test flight. The air intakes feeding the de Havilland Gyron Junior jets in these early Buccaneers were of smaller diameter than those on Mk 2 aircraft which were powered by Rolls-Royce Speys. *AE Hughes via the late Ray Sturtivant*

Boulton Paul

Boulton Paul's aircraft manufacturing history opened in Norwich in 1915 and Boulton Paul Aircraft Ltd, established in 1934, moved to Wolverhampton in 1936. Its most famous wartime product was the Defiant fighter but its major postwar aircraft programme was the Balliol trainer. The types which qualify the company for this publication were the P.111 and P.120 research aeroplanes, although the latter survived for such a short time that it appears that a colour picture was never successfully made of this airframe. Aircraft manufacture came to an end at BP in 1954, and in 1961 the company was acquired by the Dowty Group to become Dowty Boulton Paul.

Boulton Paul P.111 and P.120

In 1947 Boulton Paul began the construction of a pair of research aircraft each powered by one Rolls-Royce Nene jet. These aircraft were intended to examine the characteristics of the delta wing and the design was called the P.111, but problems with the programme meant that the first aircraft did not fly until 10 October 1950. To begin with the second airframe was expected to be almost identical but in due course it was agreed that all-moving wingtips should be fitted to this machine for control purposes. A horizontal tailplane was also introduced and as such the modified design was renamed P.120 and it first flew on 6 August 1952. However, less than a month later on 29 August the

P.120, serial VT951, was destroyed in a crash which meant it never took part in a Farnborough Show. Had it done so then colour photographs of this black painted aircraft would almost certainly have been made. The P.111 VT935 continued to perform research flights until 1957.

ABOVE The Boulton Paul P.111 research aircraft VT935 was painted in a very high visibility yellow livery after it was modified to P.111A standard. It is seen here on the flight line at RAE Bedford in June 1957. *Peter Berry*

RIGHT The P.120 development of the Boulton Paul P.111 VT951 featured a tailplane and a black colour scheme, but was lost in a crash on 29 August 1952 less than a month after its first flight. Happily, pilot Ben Gunn ejected safely. *Phil Butler*

Bristol

ABOVE The venerable wartime Bristol Beaufighter soldiered on in RAF service as a target tug until 1960. This TT.Mk 10 RD809 was spotted at RAF Benson in 1959. The black and yellow undersides signified that this aircraft was a tug. *RB Glover via Peter Green*

A very famous British aircraft company, the Bristol & Colonial Aeroplane Company was formed at Filton in 1910 by Sir George White. During the First World War and up to the mid-1930s fighters designed by Bristol equipped many RAF squadrons but by 1945 the company, which in 1920 had become the Bristol Aeroplane Co, was concentrating on larger aircraft. A series of twin-engine piston bombers and fighters – the Blenheim, Beaufort, Beaufighter, Buckingham and Brigand – were succeeded after the war by the 170 Freighter, the huge but unsuccessful Brabazon airliner, and then the beautiful Britannia airliner first flown in August 1951. The last all-Bristol design was the Type 188 supersonic research aircraft but enough examples of the Beaufighter and Brigand continued in service postwar to be pictured in colour. After having become part of BAC in 1960, today the Filton facility belongs to the hugely successful Airbus consortium.

Bristol Beaufighter
First flown on 17 July 1939, the Beaufighter was one of the most successful of Britain's wartime aircraft. Versions powered by Rolls-Royce Merlin and Bristol

RIGHT The first production Bristol TF.Mk 1 Brigand torpedo fighter was RH742 shown here which flew for the first time in 1945. This Coastal Command torpedo variant was eventually cancelled but a light bomber version did enter service. RH742 was used for trials work and Struck Off Charge in 1954.

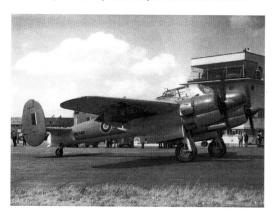

Hercules engines saw service during the conflict, especially in the night fighter role and as a torpedo bomber, but once peace had been achieved the type was considered to be obsolete. Nevertheless, some Hercules-powered aircraft operated for many more years – a few frontline units kept the aircraft until 1950 and then a number of surplus aircraft were employed as TT.Mk 10 target tugs until 1960.

Bristol Buckingham and Buckmaster
The prototype Buckingham medium bomber was flown in February 1943 and the type was put into production, but no squadrons were ever equipped with the aircraft. Problems in its development took too long to solve and then the RAF declared that it had no requirement for the type. Some of the airframes on order were converted into transports and a few Buckinghams were used for trials flying through 1945 to 1947. However, a special trainer variant called the Buckmaster was also put into production (the first prototype flew on 27 October 1944) and these airframes did find employment as pilot conversion trainers for the Brigand light bomber below. They were retired in 1958.

Bristol Brigand
The Bristol Centaurus-powered Brigand was first ordered as an RAF Coastal Command torpedo fighter and made its first flight on 4 December 1944. However, with the Second World War over, the strike wings in Coastal Command were cut back with considerable speed and suddenly there was no longer any requirement for the Brigand. In due course, however, Bristol's new aircraft was adapted as the B.Mk 1 light bomber and from 1950 to 1953 it found some particularly heavy employment flying operations with RAF units over the Malayan jungle. Another version (the Met.Mk 3) was used for meteorological work and two more (the T.Mks 4 and 5) entered service as unarmed Airborne Interception radar training aircraft. The Brigand was taken out of service in 1958.

Bristol 188
In 1952 a design competition for a research aircraft designed to fly at twice the speed of sound was won by the Bristol 188 and two examples of this stainless steel design were ordered. However, politics and problems fabricating the metal airframe brought long delays and the first machine did not fly from Filton until 14 April 1962. It was powered by a pair of de Havilland Gyron Junior engines but the aircraft suffered from a lack of power and fuel capacity and never actually reached Mach 2 – Mach 1.88 proved to be its best speed. Nevertheless, a substantial flight test programme was undertaken with the two airframes which ended in January 1964.

ABOVE The first of two Bristol 188 supersonic research aircraft XF923 is pictured at Filton on 3 April 1962 prior to carrying out some taxi trials. It made its maiden flight eleven days later. This aircraft was used for flight testing only at subsonic speeds and at moderate altitudes. *David Charlton, British Aerospace*

ABOVE The 'supersonic' Bristol 188 was XF926 which is seen here just about to land at Filton in (it is thought) early July 1963. The fin of a Hawker Hunter chase plane appears above the 188's fuselage. *David Charlton, British Aerospace*

British Aircraft Corporation (BAC)

Formed on 1 July 1960 by the merger of Bristol Aircraft, English Electric, Hunting Aircraft and Vickers-Armstrong, BAC survived for just seventeen years before it was nationalised in 1977 along with Hawker Siddeley and Scottish Aviation to form British Aerospace. Many of BAC's products fall outside the book's parameters of course but, of its various civilian airliner programmes, the supersonic Concorde which flew in March 1969 stands out. From a military point of view the most important project was the TSR.2 supersonic strike aircraft which was abandoned in 1965, but there were also successful sales of the Lightning fighter both at home and overseas (the Lightning features in the section under English Electric).

ABOVE Just the one BAC TSR.2 strike aircraft was flown (XR219) but 45 years after the programme was cancelled the machine still generates an enormous amount of interest. The ground shot has previously been used by the author but it is one of his favourites. It was taken at A&AEE Boscombe Down in 1964, probably before the aircraft had flown. *North West Heritage*

BAC TSR.2

The TSR.2 was one of the most controversial of all British aircraft, but space prevents the complex reasons behind this situation from being discussed here. The initials TSR stood for Tactical Strike and Reconnaissance and the project was initiated in 1958 as a supersonic replacement for the hugely successful English Electric Canberra bomber and multi-role aircraft. Production aircraft were ordered but the cost of the programme grew steadily until the Government cancelled the project in April 1965. At that stage just one TSR.2, with its twin Bristol Siddeley powerplant, had entered flight test having become airborne for the first time on 27 September 1964.

BAC 221

One example of the Fairey Delta II described in Chapter Three (WG774) was rebuilt with an ogee wing to serve as a high speed research aircraft for the Concorde supersonic transport. The prime objective was to test Concorde's innovative wing shape and in its rebuilt form WG774 made its first flight on 1 May 1964. A successful test programme, which included assessments of the airliner's approach and landing and development of auto-throttle equipment for approach speed stability, was concluded in 1973.

de Havilland

Some aircraft companies specialised in specific types (fighters or bombers, transports or training aeroplanes) but the world-famous de Havilland company has manufactured aircraft in many different categories (and during the 1950s and 1960s guided missiles were added to its list). The de Havilland Aircraft Company was formed in 1920 at Stag Lane but by the 1940s the firm's headquarters had moved to Hatfield. The most important post-Second World War product has to be the Comet, the world's first jet airliner which flew in 1949, but there were other small piston airliners and later the Trident jet airliner. DH's postwar activities also included the Hornet and Sea Hornet piston fighters, the Vampire, Venom and Sea Venom jet fighters, the DH.108 high speed research aircraft, and the DH.110 night fighter which was turned into the Sea Vixen all-weather fighter for the Fleet Air Arm. Much of the naval work was undertaken by de Havilland's Christchurch facility which up to 1948 had been the home of Airspeed. Fortunately, perhaps because of the need to promote the Comet to world markets, DH made use of colour film from very soon after the war. Fortunately also, not all of it was saved for the airliners because some of the military types are well covered in colour in the DH photo archive (including post-1945 examples of the Mosquito). The Christchurch factory was closed in 1962, the incomplete Sea Vixen production being moved to

DH's Chester (Hawarden) factory. Hawarden (or Broughton) was built during the war as a Vickers-Armstrong shadow factory and was acquired by de Havilland in 1948; today it belongs to Airbus UK. De Havilland became part of Hawker Siddeley in 1960 and Hatfield was closed in 1993.

de Havilland Mosquito

The world's first true multi-role combat aircraft, the outstanding all-wood structure Mosquito first became airborne on 25 November 1940. The war saw the aeroplane developed into a huge range of different fighter, bomber, reconnaissance and other versions and employment was still found for plenty of Mosquitos after 1945, much of it with overseas units. Some target-towing Mosquitos survived in RAF service until 1963.

de Havilland Hornet and Sea Hornet

Almost the last word in piston fighter development in the UK (along with the Hawker Sea Fury) the Hornet was a pilot's dream and one of the fastest piston aircraft around. Powered by the Rolls-Royce 130-Series Merlin piston engine, the prototype first flew on 28 July 1944. Hornet F.Mk 1 aircraft first joined RAF UK-based squadrons in 1946 and these were followed by the Mk 3. All home units lost their aircraft in 1951, but squadrons in Malaya and Hong Kong were re-equipped with Hornets and these stayed in service until 1955, in the process building up an impressive

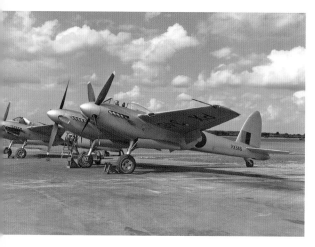

ABOVE One of the most photogenic of aeroplanes was the de Havilland Hornet fighter and the author makes no apology for including a couple of photos which have been seen before. This image presents Hornet F.Mk. 1 PX346 at Hatfield in about August 1946 and was probably taken on the same day as the PR-blue Mosquito. As an F.1, PX346 has the type's original (and better looking?) small fin. This aircraft was sold for scrap in 1951 after serving with Nos. 64 and 19 Squadrons. *BAE Systems Heritage, Farnborough*

ABOVE The Sea Hornet F.Mk 20 was the navalised version of the RAF Hornet and, like the RAF's F.Mk 3, featured an extended fin. In TT202's cockpit for a series of publicity photos taken on this sortie (made in June or July 1947) was test pilot Pat Fillingham. *BAE Systems Heritage, Farnborough*

LEFT & BELOW Sea Hornet TT202 was also photographed for publicity purposes by *The Aeroplane*, this time on the ground at RNAS Ford in about 1946. Service personnel have been posed making an inspection of their new fighter. *Aeroplane*

record of ground attack operations against Malayan terrorists. Meanwhile the Royal Navy had adopted a version which it called the Sea Hornet F.Mk 20 and then there was the modified NF.Mk 21 night fighter Sea Hornet which remained operational until 1954. The Fleet Requirements Unit in Malta flew Sea Hornets until 1957.

de Havilland Vampire

Britain's second jet fighter, the de Havilland Vampire, first flew on 20 September 1943 and after the war it went on to join a very long list of RAF Squadrons both in the UK and overseas. It was powered by the de Havilland Goblin engine and the early F.Mk 1 and 3 fighter versions were eventually succeeded by the fighter-bomber FB.Mk 5s and 9s. Built with a mix of wood and metal construction the Vampire was also sold in numbers to many other air arms (including the Fleet Air Arm) and began a development line for its manufacturer which eventually embraced a two-seat night fighter (the RAF's NF.Mk 10), trainer variants and

the follow-on Venom. The type's frontline RAF career came to a close in the late 1950s but trainer Vampires were still flying well into the 1960s and examples served abroad for many years after that.

de Havilland Venom and Sea Venom

The Venom was a development of the Vampire with a new and thinner wing plus a more powerful de Havilland Ghost engine. A first flight was achieved on 2 September 1949 and for the RAF the Venom was initially looked on as an interim fighter-bomber to fill the gap between the Gloster Meteor and the Vampire and the arrival of the new swept-wing Hawker Hunter and Supermarine Swift fighters. A logical successor to the Vampire it was built in large numbers (with some going for export) and for the RAF was produced in fighter-bomber (FB.Mks 1 and 4) and also night fighter (NF.Mks 2 and 3) versions. A few fighter-bomber Venoms lasted in RAF service until 1962. The Venom's naval career was more extensive than the Vampire's because a two-seat Sea Venom was ordered as a stop-gap until the arrival of the Sea Vixen. This flew in April 1951 and as the NF.Mk 20 began to equip front line squadrons in 1954. These were followed by FAW.Mk 21 and 22 all-weather fighter versions and the Sea Venom took part in the Suez Crisis of 1956 and remained operational into the 1960s. Service with back-up units such as the Fleet Requirements Unit kept Sea Venoms going until 1970.

ABOVE A splendid colour view of an early de Havilland Vampire F.Mk 1 fighter. The aircraft lackssquadron markings which suggests it was photographed (in about 1946/47) prior to delivery; the serial is not discernible but appears to be in the TG3xx series. *BAE Systems Heritage, Farnborough*

RIGHT A fascinating view taken at English Electric's Samlesbury factory which shows a line of brand new Vampire fighters. The nearest and fourth aircraft are in the markings and colours of the Swedish Air Force while the three RAF F.1s are TG341 (nearest), TG386 and (possibly) TG329. In Swedish service the Vampire was known as the J 28 and a first batch of seventy Mk 1 Vampires was ordered in 1946 as J 28As. These J 28As show no identity markings. *Aeroplane*

ABOVE This view of a
Swedish Mk 1 Vampire
is full of interest. The
aircraft is undergoing
ground engine running,
apparently in front
of several officials, a
vintage lorry has sneaked
into the foreground and
several Mosquitos and
Hornets sit in the
background. The Vampire's
serial is Fv28004 and
'13' is marked on the nose,
signifying that the aircraft
was allocated to F13 Wing
at Norrköping which in
1946 was the first Swedish
unit to convert to the
Vampire. The picture
is thought to have been
taken at Hatfield in early
September 1950 during
a visit by the Swedish Air
Force unit. *Aeroplane*

ABOVE De Havilland photo showing one of the company's Venom jet fighter-bombers, WE255. This aircraft was the first production FB.Mk 1 and in this early 1950s picture it is seen carrying a heavy bomb as part of some trials with this store. *BAE Systems Heritage, Farnborough*

RIGHT Besides the fighter-bomber versions of Venom, the RAF acquired a good number of two-seat night fighters in the form of the NF.Mk 2 and NF.Mk 3. The first NF.3 flew in February 1953 and this example, WX787 photographed in the mid-1950s, was used for manufacturer's trials at Boscombe Down. *BAE Systems Heritage, Farnborough*

LEFT Alongside the various combat variants a large number of two-seat DH.115 Vampire trainers were manufactured. In this late 1960s picture T.Mk 11 WZ507, with the Day-Glo stripes applied to training Vampires late in their service career, is seen on approach to land.

ABOVE LEFT AND RIGHT Although appearing to be part of a sequence of photos showing the same aircraft as the previous photo, in fact this pair of mid-1950s official images shows another NF.3. The serial is difficult to read but it appears to be WX868. *MoD*

BELOW Yet another version of the Vampire/Venom family was the Sea Venom naval all-weather fighter. Here we see an FAW.Mk 22 of No. 891 Squadron being prepared for launch from the carrier HMS *Bulwark* in 1958. A Hawker Sea Hawk is being loaded onto the right-hand catapult. *Tony Kilner*

de Havilland DH.108

The DH.108 was the first high speed research aircraft to be built in the UK to feature swept wings and, tragically, all three examples that were built were lost in fatal crashes (the last in May 1950). Essentially this was a development of the Vampire with the fighter's fuselage pod extended rearwards to provide space for a vertical fin. It was powered by a de Havilland Goblin jet. Initially, the DH.108's primary objective was to collect experience and knowledge in swept wings in readiness for the DH.106 Comet swept wing jet airliner. However, the Comet was subsequently fitted with a tailplane (something which the DH.108 did not have) but the scale model programme was continued as a pure research effort. The first DH.108 flew on 15 May 1946 and unofficially the aircraft was named Swallow.

de Havilland DH.110 and Sea Vixen

Two prototypes of the Rolls-Royce Avon-powered DH.110 RAF night fighter were built, the first flying on 26 September 1951. This first machine, however, was lost in a tragic incident at the September 1952 Farnborough Show and plans to produce the type for the Service were dropped. However, a little later the Fleet Air Arm ordered a DH.110 development which it called the Sea

LEFT The only colour images of the DH.108 seen to date by the author were those produced by Charles E. Brown. None are available for this work and so a black and white must suffice. This picture shows the third DH.108 VW120 which first flew in July 1947.

Vixen, and a third DH.110 was built as a naval prototype which flew on 20 June 1955. After joining the FAA in November 1958 the new Sea Vixen FAW.Mk 1 all-weather fighter went on to equip four frontline squadrons. In due course the modified FAW.Mk 2 with more advanced weapons was introduced and the last frontline squadron lost its Sea Vixens in January 1972. However, the Fleet Requirements Unit kept examples until 1974 while other Sea Vixens were used for trials work. A few examples converted into drones stretched the type's service career into the 1990s.

BELOW The second DH.110 prototype was WG240 which is seen here in 1952 in an all-black colour scheme. Later in 1953, when Navy interest in the type was beginning to grow, WG240 was repainted in naval colours. *BAE Systems Heritage, Farnborough*

FACING PAGE Taken at the same time in 1963/64 as the image on page 13, this pair of slides presents further angles of de Havilland Sea Vixen FAW. Mk 1 XN707 '242' of No. 890 Squadron. *Sir Mark Thomson*

ABOVE The Sea Vixen FAW. Mk 2 entered service towards the end of the period embraced by this book. This manufacturer's view shows FAW.2 prototype XN684 on 27 August 1962 piloted by test pilot Desmond Penrose. The aircraft is fitted with an extended nose pitot for calibration purposes. *BAE Systems Heritage, Farnborough*

Chapter Three
British Aircraft Companies – E to H

Continuing this survey of the major British manufacturers who were responsible for the design and development of major military aircraft, this chapter looks at a company which came relatively late into the British aircraft industry picture but which still operates today (English Electric whose facilities at Preston and Warton now produce the Eurofighter Typhoon). There is also another naval specialist who moved for a short period into high speed aeroplanes (Fairey), the first company to get involved with jet-powered aircraft (Gloster) and a world-famous fighter company (Hawker).

ABOVE English Electric Lightning F.Mk 3 XP694 was first flown on 1 May 1963 and for the early part of its career was used for various trials. This manufacturer's image was made in the mid-1960s. *BAE Systems*

English Electric

English Electric (EE) was established in 1918 and in the 1920s became responsible for some minor aircraft, but during the Second World War and for a while after the company concentrated on the manufacture of aircraft designed by other firms. The types in question where the Handley Page Hampden (a pre war bomber design) and the Halifax (below), and after these EE moved on to jet fighters in the form of the de Havilland Vampire listed in Chapter Two. This manufacturing experience, together with a decision to form a design team, eventually permitted EE to go on to produce some ground-breaking aircraft of its own. First came the Canberra, Britain's first jet bomber, and this was followed by the Lightning supersonic fighter. The next product was the unsuccessful TSR.2 strike aircraft which was developed after EE had become part of the British Aircraft Corporation in 1960 (Chapter Two), and that has since been followed by the Anglo-French SEPECAT Jaguar first flown in 1968, the multi-role Panavia Tornado with Germany and Italy (1974), the Experimental Aircraft Project or EAP (a technology demonstrator aircraft flown in 1986) and of course today the Eurofighter Typhoon with Germany, Italy and Spain which first flew in 1994.

The facilities that made up the English Electric organisation in 1945 were based at Preston and Samlesbury and during the war the latter's airfield witnessed the first flights of all of EE's bomber production. However, in 1948 the company moved its design office to Warton at an airfield which during the war had operated as an air depot of the US Army Air Force, overseeing thousands of

American aircraft on their way to various war zones. This site was turned into an experimental flying facility because the runway at Samlesbury was not long enough to handle jet-powered aircraft. All of these factories still operate today under the BAE Systems banner.

English Electric Canberra

English Electric announced its intentions with a design that, as noted above, became Britain's first jet bomber, the Canberra, although initially it was known as the A.1. The primary objective was to produce a jet-powered multi-role aircraft that would succeed and replace the de Havilland Mosquito featured in Chapter Two. Such had been the versatility of the Mosquito that having a jet-powered aircraft capable of performing similar tasks but at higher speeds was highly desirable and the resulting Canberra

ABOVE Rare colour view (a Dufay image) of the blue English Electric Canberra prototype VN799. It is pictured during the September 1949 Farnborough Show. Note the fin fillet which was later removed. *Peter Berry*

BELOW Another Canberra at Farnborough, this time B.Mk 2 WF909 in September 1957. For trials purposes this aircraft had been fitted with one de Havilland Gyron Junior engine in the port side nacelle only. *Peter Green*

was indeed produced in many versions. The prototype first flew on 13 May 1949 powered by two examples of the new Rolls-Royce Avon axial jet and the type was subsequently built in considerable numbers both for the RAF and for overseas air forces. It joined its first RAF unit in 1951 and the last British examples (equipped for photo-reconnaissance work) were finally retired in 2006.

English Electric P.1 and Lightning

Such was the pace of progress in aircraft speeds that in 1954, just nine years after the Second World War had closed, two British supersonic research aircraft made their debuts. One was the Fairey Delta 2 (below) and the other was the English Electric P.1. Although designed to a fighter specification the P.1 was built primarily to serve as a supersonic research aircraft (perhaps in today's jargon as a technology demonstrator) and the first of two examples flew on 4 August 1954. Both were powered by two Armstrong Siddeley Sapphire axial jets and they provided vital experience and data for supersonic flight. Very soon a much redesigned development was produced called the P.1B. The Rolls-Royce Avon-powered P.1B became the prototype of Britain's first supersonic fighter and first flew on 4 April 1957. In due course it was called the Lightning and the type eventually proved capable of Mach 2 and served with the RAF in six versions; a larger fin was one of the differences exhibited by later upgraded aircraft. The Lightning, which was always a great favourite with its pilots, also joined the air forces of Saudi Arabia and Kuwait and the last RAF examples were retired in 1988.

A spectacular night
view of English Electric
Lightning XM145 in 1962
with the reheat system
of its two Avon engines
undergoing ground
running. At the time the
aircraft was serving as
aircraft 'Q' of No. 74
Squadron. *BAE Systems
via Joe Cherrie*

ABOVE Later marks of Lightning required an increase to their fin area to counteract the extra weight of the new Red
Top air-to-air missiles that they carried and the installation of a large ventral fuel tank. The eventual choice was a
larger, squared-off fin but in the early 1960s XA847, the first P.1B prototype, was modified with this fin fillet
extension as a trial. *BAE Systems*

Fairey

ABOVE Fairey Firefly F.Mk 1 PP481 '278/P' seen aboard the carrier HMS *Triumph* in the early months of 1950. At the time it was flying with No. 827 Squadron, but the 'VL' fin code from its previous base at Yeovilton is still visible – painted over in 'clean' white paint on the fin beneath the 'P'. On 10 March 1950 PP481 entered *Triumph's* barrier and was damaged beyond repair.

Fairey Aviation was founded in 1915 by Richard Fairey. During the Second World War and after 1945 the company specialised to a degree in naval aircraft, for example with the famous Swordfish torpedo bomber. Fairey's main factory was built at Hayes in Middlesex but in 1935 a new manufacturing works at Heaton Chapel near Manchester was acquired to cope with the military workload. The flight test facilities for Heaton Chapel were housed at Ringway Airport at Manchester, while the Fireflies and Gannets discussed below were taken from Hayes and flown from Fairey's flight test base at White Waltham airfield. Postwar the firm also experimented with high performance jet aircraft, work that reached its peak with the Delta 2 research type. Also during the 1950s there were some helicopter projects which culminated in the Rotodyne vertical take-off airliner, but none of these proved successful. In 1960 Fairey's aviation interests were merged with Westland Aircraft, but the name and the Heaton Chapel factory survived for some years as Fairey Engineering, producing items such as the Medium Girder Bridge for military and civil use.

Fairey Firefly

The only wartime Fairey product to see prolonged service after 1945 was the Firefly naval aircraft. The first prototype had flown on 22 December 1941 and by 1945 the Firefly had completed a substantial operational service record. Postwar fighter-bomber versions of the aircraft equipped a number of FAA squadrons and performed regular strike and ground attack operations over Korea during the war of 1950 to 1953, and also over Malaya in 1954. Other versions served as anti-submarine aircraft or target tugs and in 1952 work began on producing a target drone based on the Firefly. In due course many Fireflies were converted into target drones after their withdrawal. The last aircraft operated by the Royal Navy were retired in the mid-1950s, but those with the Royal Australian Navy and some of the six other air arms to receive Fireflies stayed in service for rather longer, in some cases well into the 1960s.

RIGHT More Fairey Fireflies overseas, this time serving with the Royal Australian Navy (RAN). The picture shows the AS.Mk 6 anti-submarine variant which equipped No. 851 Squadron. They are flying off the east coast of New South Wales in 1956 and the nearest aircraft has the code '274' but its serial is unreadable. *David Eagles*

ABOVE Just the one example of the not very handsome Fairey Delta 1 research aircraft was flown and in the air it was not the most pleasant machine to fly.

Fairey Spearfish

A massive torpedo bomber, the first Spearfish prototype made its maiden flight on 5 July 1945. Production orders were subsequently cancelled and only four examples flew (the last in September 1947) but in 1952 one of these was still being used for trials flying. No colour images of the Spearfish have been traced to date.

Fairey Delta 1

The sole example of this stocky compact delta wing research aircraft became airborne on 12 March 1951 (work on a second prototype was abandoned). The Fairey Delta 1 featured a high polish metal finish and was powered by one Rolls-Royce Derwent jet engine.

It proved to be a difficult aircraft to fly and was never held in high reputation, but its flight programme did run until February 1956. The author has no colour views of this aircraft.

Fairey Gannet

A postwar requirement for a new carrier-based anti-submarine aircraft was met by the portly Fairey Gannet, the first prototype of which began its flight testing on 19 September 1949. The type's full service entry was delayed until 1955 but the Gannet proved successful and further variants were developed including a heavily modified airborne early warning (AEW) aircraft. Examples were also acquired by the Australian and German navies and the Indonesian armed forces. The last FAA examples were retired in December 1978 following the withdrawal of the carrier HMS *Ark Royal*.

ABOVE The Royal Australian Navy bought examples of the Fairey Gannet AS.Mk 1 anti-submarine aircraft. The nearest aircraft in this view, XA327 '976/Y', was delivered in August 1955 but when this photo was taken in 1957 it was still waiting to receive its Australian Navy roundels and code. These aircraft were based at RNAS Nowra and the photo was taken off the coast of New South Wales (although the 'Y' signifies the carrier HMAS *Melbourne* as XA327's home). *David Eagles*

LEFT The Fairey Gannet AEW.Mk 3 was externally quite different to the previous anti-submarine versions and this image shows XL495 '425/V' of No. 849B Squadron serving with HMS *Victorious* but seen here at Hal Far in Malta. Delivered in October 1960, this aircraft had a very short career because it was written off on 22 November 1960. *AE Hughes via the late Ray Sturtivant*

Fairey Delta 2

Two examples of the supersonic delta-wing Fairey Delta 2 research aircraft powered by a single Rolls-Royce Avon were ordered in 1950 and the first of these (WG774) made its maiden flight on 6 August 1954. On 10 March 1956 this aeroplane, flying over the south of England, smashed the World Air Speed Record in setting an average figure of 1,132.2mph (1,821.7km/h) - one of the finest achievements of British aviation history. WG774 was withdrawn in 1960 to be converted into the BAC 221 (Chapter Two) but the second airframe WG777 continued flying until 1966. The Delta 2's research programme proved very successful and during the 1950s Fairey proposed several fighter projects based on the type, but none of these were ordered.

ABOVE On 10 March 1956 the Fairey Delta 2 WG774 broke the World Air Speed Record. Prior to the SBAC Farnborough Show in September 1957 the aircraft had been repainted in this mauve colour scheme with 'Holder of World Absolute Speed Record' painted in white lettering on the sides of the forward fuselage. Note that the droop nose is lowered. *Peter Berry*

RIGHT This picture of Delta 2 WG774 was taken in the late 1950s when the aircraft was flying with RAE. *Clive Rustin*

RIGHT Views of the Delta 2 WG777 are less common than for WG774 but this example shows the second aircraft at RAE Bedford in June 1957 parked alongside one of the English Electric P.1s WG763. For the author the blue scheme with natural metal nose is rather more attractive than WG774's rather 'loud' mauve effort. *Peter Berry*

Folland Aircraft Ltd at Hamble was named after its designer Henry Folland, who had left his post with Gloster Aircraft after the control of that firm was taken over by Hawker in 1934. In fact Folland Aircraft was formed in 1937 out of the former British Marine

Folland

Aircraft Ltd and during its relatively short existence (Folland became part of Hawker Siddeley in 1960) the company was responsible for flying just one type of fighter, the lightweight Gnat jet fighter. In due course that aeroplane was turned into a more successful two-seat trainer. In 1953 Folland established a flight development unit at Chilbolton airfield for the Gnat, staying until 1961.

Folland Midge and Gnat

The Gnat was started as a very light fighter project and the private venture Folland Fo.139 Midge airframe, a preliminary Gnat 'prototype' fitted with an Armstrong Siddeley Viper 101 engine, flew on 11 August 1954. The Fo.141 Gnat itself, an incredibly small jet fighter, was powered by a Bristol Orpheus 701 and the first of a development batch of six aircraft flew on 18 July 1955. The RAF rejected the fighter but a trainer version was ordered which famously went on to equip the *Red Arrows* aerobatic display team. Both fighter and trainer versions were used by overseas air forces and the Indian manufacturer Hindustan Aeronautics built the single-seat fighter Gnat under licence. In the 1970s Hindustan introduced an improved Gnat which it called the Ajeet.

LEFT Although a small development batch of Gnat F.Mk 1s was delivered to the RAF the fighter was not adopted for service use. However, the two-seat trainer was, and from 1965 it equipped the *Red Arrows* display team. For the 1964 season a five-aircraft Gnat aerobatics team was formed at RAF Valley called the *Yellowjacks* and this Russell Adams view shows the team in practice. *Jet Age Museum*

Gloster

This company began its life in 1917 as the Gloucestershire Aircraft Co but in 1926 it was renamed Gloster Aircraft. It came under the control of Hawker Aircraft in 1934, and consequently part of Hawker Siddeley in 1935, and its base factory and airfield was situated at Brockworth just south of Cheltenham (the works was also known as Hucclecote since it came very close to the parish of that name). A specialist in RAF fighters throughout its existence, during the Second World War Gloster became the first British company to build jet-powered aircraft with the E.28/39 research type and then the Meteor fighter. The latter's production continued well into the 1950s and was succeeded by the huge Javelin all-weather fighter. The Javelin proved to be Gloster's last aircraft and, since the type was too large to operate out of the Brockworth airfield, production machines were flown out of Moreton Valence, an RAF field just a few miles away which Glosters had been using as a flight test facility since 1943. Also during the war Glosters established a design and experimental establishment at Bentham a couple of miles from Brockworth. In 1962, two years after becoming part of the company mergers into Hawker Siddeley, the Brockworth factory and Moreton Valence airfield were closed. A little later the latter's runway disappeared beneath the M5 motorway.

LEFT During the later part of its flying career the surviving Gloster E.28/39 W4041 had small finlets fitted to the outer part of each horizontal tailplane. However, in readiness for public display during 1945 the aircraft was refurbished and the finlets were removed.

Gloster E.28/39

Strictly speaking, the E.28/39 research aircraft does not qualify for inclusion because it first flew (most famously) in May 1941 as Britain's first jet aeroplane and its flying career came to a close in 1945 before the war was over. Two examples were built and one was lost in a crash in 1943, but the other (W4041) survives today as a museum exhibit having completed a very successful flight test programme. However, during the summer of 1945 this aircraft did feature in a postwar Ministry exhibition in Oxford Street in London, and later it was exhibited in the centres of Gloucester and Cheltenham, and a colour view of W4041 is available.

In 1946 Gloster modified an F.Mk IV Meteor into a demonstration aircraft which was painted red and received the civil registration G-AIDC. This picture from the *Aeroplane* collection was taken by Charles Brown on 12 April 1947. In May 1947 G-AIDC crashed in Belgium and the airframe was subsequently rebuilt into the T. Mk 7 demonstrator G-AKPK shown on page 7. *Aeroplane*

Gloster Meteor

The twin-engine Meteor was Britain's first jet fighter and first flew on 3 March 1943. It made a small contribution to the war effort but the major part of its career came after 1945 when updated and more capable variants steadily became available. In due course the fighter was built in large numbers both for the RAF and for quite a number of overseas air arms. The major postwar single-seat Meteor variants were the F.Mks 4 and 8 with Rolls-Royce Derwent jets but the fighter reconnaissance FR.Mk 9 and photo-reconnaissance PR.Mk 10 also completed valuable careers. There was also the two-seat T.Mk 7 trainer and in addition the Meteor's twin wing-mounted engine configuration permitted a good number of airframes to be used as test beds for alternative powerplants. Although many RAF Meteors were withdrawn during the 1950s some versions did last into the 1960s. Gloster's preoccupation with all of these variants for home and export meant that Armstrong Whitworth would take on the responsibility of the two-seat night fighter Meteors (see Chapter Two).

LEFT One of the famous Russell Adams 'aircraft in a loop' aerobatic photos. Here we see a Meteor FR. Mk 9 VW360, a version that was identical to the F.Mk 8 fighter apart from oblique cameras mounted in its nose. *Jet Age Museum*

ABOVE AND LEFT The Meteor FR.Mk 9 was ordered by the Ecuadorean Air Force and these images show serial 712 during a test flight before it was delivered to Ecuador. On this aircraft the camera ports have been covered by temporary metal panels. *Jet Age Museum*

LEFT This Meteor T.Mk 7 SE-DCC is seen at Glosters awaiting delivery to Svenskä Flygtjänst AB, a contractor who provided target-towing for the armed forces of both Sweden and Denmark. As a T.7 this aircraft had previously been another Gloster demonstrator, the blue-painted G-ANSO, and before that the single-seater 'Reaper' private venture ground attack prototype. A Javelin is parked behind. *Jet Age Museum*

RIGHT Many Meteors were used as flight test beds for new and different jet engines. One of the most well known was WA820 which had a pair of Armstrong Siddeley Sapphire engines installed in 1950. These were far more powerful than the fighter's standard units and required larger nacelles. WA820 was shown at the 1950 and 1951 SBAC Displays at Farnborough. *Jet Age Museum*

RIGHT Gloster E.1/44 Ace TX145 photographed at Moreton Valence in November 1947. *Bill Baldwin via Jet Age Museum*

LEFT Gloster Meteor T.Mk 7 two-seat trainer WA602 is photographed coming into land at Lyneham in 1961. *Peter Green*

Gloster E.1/44 Ace

There appear to be no colour photos of this prototype fighter which, with its single Rolls-Royce Nene centrifugal jet housed inside the fuselage, has always made an interesting comparison to the Meteor. This is a pity, but then in many respects the Ace was not an outstanding aircraft anyway. Three examples were built but only two flew, with the first making its flight debut on 9 March 1948, much later than originally predicted. The Gloster Ace's flying career ended in 1951. There were plans for a production run but these were quickly abandoned.

Gloster Javelin

The prototype of this heavy two-seat all-weather fighter for the RAF made its maiden flight on 26 November 1951 powered by a pair of Armstrong Siddeley Sapphires. A difficult development programme and some poor flying characteristics delayed the type's entry into service until 1956, and in due course nine versions were produced including a dual-control trainer. Despite its problems the Javelin was to equip plenty of RAF Squadrons before its air defence role was gradually taken over by the English Electric Lightning. The last aircraft left the front line in 1968 and Gloster failed to win any export orders for the type. With its distinct delta wing the Javelin, the world's first twin-jet delta aircraft, was dubbed the 'Flying Flat Iron' or 'Flying Triangle'.

ABOVE Serial XA631 was a Gloster Javelin FAW.Mk 4 which flew for the first time in 1956. It is shown here early in its career completing a winter scene at Moreton Valence, and later in 1956 it went to A&AEE Boscombe Down for trials. Note the variant's pen nib fairing around the jet pipes.
Jet Age Museum

LEFT The Javelin T.Mk 3 prototype WT841 comes into land at Farnborough during the 1956 Show. A big difference on the trainer from the fighter Javelins was the lack of the usual large nose radome.

LEFT There were nine different versions of the Gloster Javelin and this Russell Adams view shows two of them. Nearest is XA635, an early FAW.Mk 4, with behind XA552, an early FAW.Mk 1 which has a slightly different radome. The Mk 4 also introduced an all-moving tailplane.
Jet Age Museum

LEFT AND BELOW Another chance to compare Javelins. The first shot shows Mk 4 XA635 again, while the second introduces XH966, the prototype FAW.Mk 8 which first flew on 9 May 1958. The changes included reheat for the Sapphire engines, while XH966 is also shown carrying 'empty' underwing weapons pylons and the type's 'bosom' under-fuselage fuel tanks. Neither aircraft displays any unit markings and so must still have been in the hands of the manufacturer.
Jet Age Museum

Handley Page

Founded in 1909 by Frederick Handley Page, Handley Page Ltd (HP) became famous during the First World War for big bomber designs. This reputation was sustained in the 1930s by which time the company was also producing civil airliners. The most important product during the Second World War was the Halifax bomber, examples of which continued to serve for some years after the conflict had ended. The cessation of hostilities permitted HP to return to civil airliner design with the Hermes which flew in 1945. There was also the Marathon airliner which in fact was a Miles Aircraft project taken over by Handley Page in 1948 (together with its production facility at Woodley) after Miles had gone bankrupt; the new acquisition was renamed Handley Page Reading. The company's own works were situated at Cricklewood in North London with a factory and airfield at Radlett. In the 1950s HP returned to bomber production with the Victor V-Bomber and its last product was the Jetstream regional airliner. Handley Page did not join the 1960 programme of mergers, remaining independent until the company went into liquidation in 1970.

Handley Page Halifax

The Halifax first flew in October 1939 with a Rolls-Royce Merlin powerplant but the more capable versions of the bomber were powered by the Bristol Hercules, the first example with this engine flying in October 1942. It was the Hercules Halifax which was retained in service after 1945. Primarily a bomber of course, other versions were developed and meteorological and Coastal Command

Halifaxes continued to serve the RAF until the aircraft was officially declared obsolete in 1951. Further airframes were adapted for civil use and indeed a full civil airliner conversion called the Halton also saw limited postwar service.

Handley Page HP.88

This was a scale model research aircraft designed to check out the aerodynamics and performance of the Victor's crescent wing. Two HP.88s were ordered but only the one was completed, flying on 21 June 1951. Tragically, on 26 August 1951 when flying at low level this aircraft (serial VX330) broke apart and killed its pilot. Few pictures of the aeroplane were taken in the short time of its existence, and apparently none in colour, a shame since it was painted in a royal blue colour scheme. The HP.88 had the probably unique distinction of receiving four 'names'. Handley Page subcontracted the project to General Aircraft who allocated their GAL.63 designation. In 1948 General was acquired by Blackburn and the new 'owners' renamed it Y.B.2, and in addition the aircraft used a fuselage from the Supermarine Type 510 (Chapter Four), so Supermarine called it their Type 521.

Handley Page Victor

Handley Page's most famous postwar product was the Victor medium bomber which formed one part of the V-Bomber triad of Avro Vulcan, HP Victor and Vickers Valiant. The Victor featured the then unique crescent wing with its maximum sweep angle on the innermost wing section combined with a steadily reduced amount of sweep further out along the surface. The first prototype was flown on 24 December 1952 and the type entered service in 1957, two versions eventually equipping eight squadrons. The B.Mk 1 was powered by Sapphire turbojets while the B.Mk 2 had the much more powerful Rolls-Royce Conway turbofan. The type went on to become the longest lived of the three V-Bombers staying in service (as a tanker) until 1993, and in its tanker role it made major contributions to both the 1982 Falklands War and the Gulf War in 1991.

ABOVE The second Victor prototype WB775 was given another attractive colour scheme, this time in pale blue. Here the aircraft is photographed at Farnborough during the SBAC Display of September 1955.
Richard Curtis

RIGHT The first few production Victors had an aluminium finish, but soon afterwards this was changed to all-white, as shown here by B.Mk 1 XA936 of No. 10 Squadron in 1958/59.
MoD

ABOVE Another Mk 1 Victor, XA930 was used by A&AEE and the manufacturers for trials work which included RATOG tests with de Havilland. It was in 1963, six years after its maiden flight, that the aircraft first joined an RAF Squadron.

RIGHT XH670 was a very early example of the Handley Page Victor B.Mk 2. This aircraft first flew in 1959 and was used for many trials programmes throughout the 1960s. Note the 'Küchemann carrot' streamlined fairing on the wing trailing edge which appeared only on Mk 2 aircraft. These provided space for additional equipment while reducing drag at near sonic speeds and were named after the famous scientist Dr Küchemann of RAE Farnborough.

Handley Page HP.115

The relatively simple HP.115 research aircraft was built to assess the low speed characteristics of the Concorde supersonic transport and complemented the BAC 221 described in the previous chapter (which covered the high speed part of the programme).

Just one HP.115 airframe was built and this made its maiden flight on 17 August 1961, and it went on to complete a most valuable and successful flying programme which continued up until August 1973. By that time the aircraft had made over one thousand flights.

ABOVE A Victor Mk 2 completes a flypast at the 1964 Farnborough Show. *Peter Green*

LEFT The Handley Page HP.115 low speed research aircraft was a visitor to the 1964 Farnborough Show and is seen here performing a flyover. *Graham Hopkin*

Hawker

ABOVE TOP The first marks of Hawker Tempest to enter service during the Second World War were powered by the Napier Sabre engine. Long term trials were undertaken with an annular radiator to improve the cooling efficiency and this view from 1945 shows Mk V NV768 in the foreground with the new radiator. The Mk V behind, EJ283, has the original chin arrangement. *Aeroplane*

ABOVE Hawker Tempest TT.Mk V NV704 is seen at Sylt in 1953/54 ready to receive an air test after an engine change. TT signifies Target Tug, this aircraft having been converted from its original fighter configuration. *Alan Smith via Roger Lindsay*

A truly famous company with a name secured by the wartime exploits of its Hurricane fighter. In fact H. G. Hawker Engineering Co Ltd was created in 1920 from the ashes of the famous First World War Sopwith Company and in 1933 the firm was renamed Hawker Aircraft Ltd. In 1935 Hawker became a founder member of the Hawker Siddeley Aircraft Co Ltd and the Hurricane made its first flight in the same year. That famous fighter was followed by the Typhoon in 1940, the Tempest and Sea Fury piston fighters which both served post war, the Sea Hawk naval jet fighter, the splendid Hunter swept-wing fighter, and finally the P.1127 research aircraft which opened the story of the Harrier. This list of names has become folklore in British aviation history. The main factory was first housed at Kingston near London while another major factory and the firm's wartime airfield were based at Langley near Slough. Langley saw the first flights of all of Hawker's post-Hurricane piston fighters but the factory on that site was closed in 1958. After the war it acquired another factory at Squires Gate alongside Blackpool airfield which was used for manufacturing Hunters until the late 1950s (when it was switched to general manufacturing). In 1950 the airfield at Dunsfold was acquired and eventually turned into a final assembly and test facility for the P.1127 and Harrier family (and also the 1970s Hawk jet trainer). After 1960 Hawker formed a crucial element of the reformed Hawker Siddeley Group, but Kingston and Dunsfold were closed in the 1990s.

Hawker Tempest

Versions of the Hawker Tempest were powered by either the Napier Sabre or Bristol Centaurus piston engines. The prototype flew on 2 September 1942 and it was the Sabre versions that left their mark during the Second World War. Some of these stayed in service after 1945, the Sabre F.Mk VI for instance serving at Khormaksar as late as 1950. The Centaurus-powered Tempest II first flew on 28 June 1943 and postwar this version equipped ten RAF squadrons, operating for example with units in RAF Germany and then in Malaya where they performed ground attack operations against terrorists. Many production examples of the F.Mk II also joined the Royal Indian and Royal Pakistan Air Forces.

Hawker Sea Fury

Like the Tempest, prototypes of the Hawker Fury were flown with Napier Sabre and Bristol Centaurus engines, and also the Rolls-Royce Griffon. The first Fury prototype (powered by a Centaurus) was flown on 1 September 1944 but the RAF dropped its order for Furys. However, the Navy ordered a large number

LEFT The serial of this Hawker Fury/Sea Fury prototype is not visible, but the position of the yellow 'P' prototype marking on the fuselage side ahead of the roundel suggests it is almost certainly Sea Fury SR666. The venue is Farnborough and the year 1946, SR666 having visited RAE in June and July for an exhibition. *Aeroplane*

LEFT Hawker Sea Fury WM479 '106/NW' of No. 805 Squadron Royal Australian Navy based at Nowra. The picture dates from 1957/58. *David Eagles*

of Centaurus-powered Sea Furys for the Fleet Air Arm and the aircraft built a fine career with superb service during the Korean War. FAA Sea Furys stayed in the front line until the mid-1950s and versions of the aircraft also flew with several overseas air arms. The Sea Fury was a beautiful aircraft to fly and, along with the de Havilland Hornet in Chapter Two, it was one of the fastest around in the final days of piston fighters.

Hawker P.1040 and Sea Hawk

This single-seat jet fighter was rejected by the RAF but was then bought by the Royal Navy and also West Germany and India. The first of three P.1040 prototypes first flew on 2 September 1947 and Sea Hawk F.Mk 1 fighters, powered by a Rolls-Royce Nene engine, entered FAA service in 1953. From a British point of view the career highlight was action during the Suez

ABOVE LEFT Manufacturer's photo of Hawker Sea Hawk F.Mk 1 WF159. The aircraft has no unit markings and was probably taken in 1953.

ABOVE RIGHT Sea Hawk FGA.Mk 4 WV836 '117/B' of No. 801 Squadron is seen in the late 1950s about to be loaded onto the catapult in readiness for launching. *Tony Kilner*

LEFT A brand new Sea Hawk for the Indian Navy, IN167, stands at Bitteswell before delivery. One of the very last Sea Hawks to be built, this aircraft made its maiden flight on 21 March 1961. *Ray Williams*

Crisis in 1956, plus the formation of some aerobatic teams, before the type was retired from the front line during 1960. Later versions were classed as 'FGA' to reflect the addition of ground attack capability. The best known display team was perhaps *The Red Devils* formed in 1957 by 736 Squadron, which had its aircraft painted in bright red. The fighter stayed with FAA second line units for some time beyond 1960, however, and with the Indian Navy until 1983. Pilots found the Sea Hawk a delight to fly.

Hawker P.1052 and P.1081

Two P.1052 research aircraft were ordered as swept-wing developments of the Sea Hawk, at least with the main wing swept back although the tailplane and rear fuselage were at this stage unaffected. Still powered by a Nene engine, the first P.1052 VX272 flew on 19 November 1948 and performed research and development flying until the mid-1950s, which included deck trials on the carrier HMS *Eagle* in 1952. The second aircraft VX279 flew in April 1949 but in 1950 the rear fuselage of this airframe was replaced with an all-through jetpipe and swept tailplane. As the P.1081 VX279 flew in its new form on 19 June 1950, but on 3 April 1951 the aircraft was destroyed in a fatal crash. Charles Brown and *Flight* took pictures of the P.1052 in colour but no such images have been found of the attractive P.1081.

ABOVE After their retirement from the front line Sea Hawks were flown by civilian pilots of the Fleet Requirements Unit (FRU). One of the most important FRU duties was to make dummy attacks against new and recommissioned warships as part of their radar and gun crew training. FRADU's Sea Hawks were painted black and this view shows XE339 in 1968. *Adrian Balch*

LEFT The Hawker P.1052 research aircraft was a Sea Hawk fitted with a swept wing, and the modified P.1081 introduced a swept tailplane and all-through jetpipe. The sole P.1081 VX279 may not have been photographed in colour – a pity since the aircraft had an attractive overall gloss duck-egg green livery.

BELOW An early production Hawker Hunter F.Mk 4, WT748. This aircraft first flew on 3 March 1955 and went on to join No. 118 Squadron, the lack of unit markings suggesting the picture was made in 1955 before delivery. *MoD*

Hawker Hunter

Following on from the Sea Hawk/P.1052/P.1081 line, Hawker developed the P.1067 single-seat jet fighter powered by a single Rolls-Royce Avon. The prototype P.1067 made its maiden flight on 20 July 1951 and for RAF service the type was named Hunter. This proved to be an immensely successful aircraft with sales to many

nations all over the world and over many years, some of which retained their machines until quite recently. Many frontline RAF squadrons were equipped with Hunters from the mid-1950s into the 1970s, first as a day fighter and later as a ground attack aircraft, and examples were also used by the Royal Navy by its training and support units. There were also

ABOVE Although originating from Hawker sources, this beautiful photograph of another F.Mk 4 Hunter WV325 was almost certainly taken by Gloster's Russell Adams. His archive of black and white images show views of the same aircraft taken on the same occasion in late summer 1955, at which point the aircraft was flying as 'C' with the Central Flying School (CFS). *The late Mike Stroud*

LEFT This Hunter, coded '151', was photographed at an airbase open day, probably Cottesmore, during the late 1950s while serving with the Air Fighting Development Squadron. *Graham Hopkin*

LEFT Many Hawker Hunters were operated by experimental and trials units, some with very non-standard colour schemes. This aircraft XE531 was built as a single-seat F.Mk 6 fighter, but by 1964 had been converted into the sole two-seat T.Mk 12 aircraft and was serving with RAE in this green and white scheme. The upper nose bulge was added to make room to fit trials equipment for the TSR.2 development programme. In the far distance behind the nosewheel is a Hawker P.1127 or Kestrel, dating the picture to the mid to late 1960s. *The late Mike Stroud*

BELOW The very first Hawker P.1127 prototype XP831 is pictured hovering over the Hawker Siddeley test airfield at Dunsfold. *The late Mike Stroud*

reconnaissance and trainer versions and indeed the aircraft provided the capability to fulfil many tasks in the early years of the swept-wing age within one basic airframe, in much the same way as the Gloster Meteor had done with the first generation of jet fighters. The Hunter was a beautiful aircraft to look at (the author could have filled the book with Hunter photos) and again was superb to fly.

Hawker P.1127

By the late 1950s there was growing interest in developing a combat aircraft capable of making vertical take-offs and landings (VTOL). From a British point of view this effort culminated in the creation of the Hawker P.1127 VTOL research aircraft powered by the unique Bristol BE.53 Pegasus engine fitted with rotating nozzles to provide vectored thrust. Six P.1127s were built and the first made an initial tethered hovering flight on 21 October 1960. A maiden conventional flight followed on 13 March 1961, and later that year the P.1127 completed successful transitions from a vertical take-off to wing-borne flight and back to make a vertical landing. The six aeroplanes were used as development aircraft for military research and the programme went so well that a more capable version was subsequently ordered as the Hawker Siddeley Kestrel described below. Some of the P.1127s completed long flying careers, two of them into the 1970s.

Hawker Siddeley

The name Hawker Siddeley actually relates to two organisations, the one eventually replacing the other. The 1935 formation of the Hawker Siddeley Aircraft Co Ltd brought together Armstrong Whitworth, Avro, Gloster and Hawker (and also Armstrong Siddeley Motors, Air Service Training and High Duty Alloys). Although the constituent aircraft companies were free to continue to produce their own designs under their own name (often with great success) this move provided the opportunity to share manufacturing work across the group members. For example, during the Second World War Gloster built large numbers of Hawker Hurricanes and Typhoons at a factory at Stoke Orchard near Cheltenham, and in the 1950s Armstrong Whitworth manufactured Hawker Sea Hawks and Hunters and Gloster Meteors and Javelins. The overall name was changed to Hawker Siddeley Group in 1948.

A new Hawker Siddeley Group was formed on 1 July 1960 by the merger of some of the individual companies as part of a government-driven reorganisation of the industry. Now Avro, Armstrong Whitworth, Blackburn, de Havilland, Folland, Gloster and Hawker were blended into one company and in doing so lost their individual names. In July 1963 the Group was split into Hawker Siddeley Aviation (HSA) and Hawker Siddeley Dynamics (HSD), the latter taking away the guided missile and space technology parts of the business. In 1977 Hawker Siddeley became part of the nationalised British Aerospace together with the British Aircraft Corporation and Scottish Aviation, and today this is called BAE Systems. Apart from the ongoing Kestrel/Harrier developments, and the Nimrod maritime patrol and anti-submarine aircraft that entered service in 1969, HSA's major new aircraft programmes were all civil related (e.g. the Trident airliner and HS.125 business jet). Nimrod is really an aircraft of the modern era and cannot be included

LEFT TOP Although P.1127 is painted on its nose this aircraft, XS688, is in fact the first Hawker Siddeley Kestrel trials aeroplane. The roundels represent the Tripartite Evaluation Squadron (TES) which in 1965 assessed the type very thoroughly and laid down many rules for the operation of vertical take-off and landing aircraft. *The late Mike Stroud*

LEFT CENTRE One of the Kestrel development aircraft, XS690, pictured in 1965 with the TES code 'O' painted on its nose. *Peter Green*

LEFT Another TES Kestrel XS695 code '5' photographed in the hover. At the start of their careers, all Kestrels (and the original P.1127s) had a natural metal finish. *John Farley*

here and in fact in its original form the aircraft has only recently been taken out of service. However, production of the Blackburn Buccaneer was also continued well into the 1970s.

Hawker Siddeley Kestrel and Harrier

The P.1127/Kestrel/Harrier story stretches right across the date boundaries that witnessed the final disappearance of Hawker Aircraft into Hawker Siddeley Aviation. Consequently, the follow-on Kestrel programme comes under the HSA banner. Nine more P.1127s were ordered but with modifications that absorbed and reflected much of what had been learnt with the original aircraft. These were designated Kestrel FGA.Mk 1 and the military classification was necessary because they were intended to operate with a Tripartite Evaluation Squadron (TES) that included pilots from Britain, America and West Germany. The first Kestrel flew on 7 March 1964 and the TES trials programme with the Kestrel ran from April to November 1965. Six Kestrels subsequently went to America as XV-6As for more trials work while the Tripartite Squadron experience contributed to the ordering of the Harrier attack aircraft for the RAF. The Harrier, which needs no introduction to enthusiasts and the great majority of the public, first flew on 31 August 1966 and entered service in 1969.

Hunting

jet flap blowing air out so fast through the back of the full span of the wing that the oncoming air would consider it to be one large mechanical flap, thereby artificially increasing the wing area. In its research task the H.126 proved a success and the aircraft was used by RAE until 1967 when its flying career ended. However, the airframe was subsequently taken to the NASA (National Aeronautics and Space Administration) Center at Ames in America where it was tested in a large wind tunnel. XN714 arrived home in 1970. In the end the jet flap was not adopted by civil aviation, in part because an alternative, much simpler and very effective leading edge/trailing edge flap arrangement provided modern airliners with a reduced take-off run.

LEFT The Hunting H.126 seen flying through rather misty conditions during the summer of 1965.
Clive Rustin

Hunting is a minor player in this work but was responsible for one fascinating research aircraft, the H.126 jet-flap project. Prior to 1954 this company had been named Percival Aircraft but it had been part of the Hunting Group since 1944. It was responsible for a series of light aircraft, transports and trainers, culminating in the Provost and Jet Provost basic trainers for the RAF. From 1954 the company was called Hunting Percival Ltd and from 1957 just Hunting Aircraft Ltd, and then in 1960 it was merged into BAC. The factory was based at Luton Airport.

Hunting H.126

The H.126 XN714 first flew on 26 March 1963 and was powered by a single Bristol Orpheus jet engine. This landmark took place after Hunting had become part of BAC, but in fact the design and development programme had been under way since 1958. This very unusual aircraft was created to explore the low speed handling characteristics of the 'jet flap' wing and its value in providing propulsion and additional lift. At the time there were potential applications on future jet airliners with the

ABOVE The Hunting H.126 and the Handley Page HP.115 (behind) are pictured making their way across the English Channel on 9 June 1965 during the journey to the Paris Air Show at Le Bourget. Both of these machines were low speed research aircraft with limited range and getting them to Paris proved to be quite a complex operation. Clive Rustin was piloting the HP.115 while Desmond 'Dizzy' Addicott flew the H.126.
Clive Rustin

Chapter Four
British Aircraft Companies – I to Z

This chapter rounds off the book's survey of British fighter and bomber companies and their designs. In this section we have two firms which prior to 1945 had built reputations in the field of flying boats (Saunders-Roe and Shorts), the organisation responsible for the world's most famous fighter but which also worked on flying boats and seaplanes (Supermarine with the Spitfire of course), another bomber and large aircraft specialist (Vickers) and a company which still survives as a world leader in helicopter development (Westland). Some other important British aircraft companies might have featured here had they produced fighters and bombers. During the Second World War Miles and Martin-Baker did build some fighter prototypes and the most important of them featured (quite famously) in air displays after 1945 and was still flying in December 1947. The aircraft in question was the Martin-Baker M.B.5 piston fighter first flown in May 1944, but sadly the author has never seen a colour photo of that superb aeroplane. It was after that project that Martin-Baker moved on to its enormously successful business in developing ejection seats for high speed aircraft.

Although the objective here has been to provide a brief listing of the main aircraft manufacturers, it should not be forgotten that the various engine companies – Armstrong Siddeley, Bristol, de Havilland, Napier and Rolls-Royce – became involved in a lot of important flight test and trials programmes. Many aircraft were allocated to help with these, often taking on new and individual colour schemes of their own, and a few appear in these pages. There were also organisations like Flight Refuelling Ltd in Dorset, which today carries the name of its founder Alan Cobham as Cobham plc. Although a private company, FRL as it was often known was involved in plenty of important trials and conversion projects on many fighter and bomber types.

**ABOVE Vickers Valiant XD873 was one of the last production examples to be completed.
It is shown here making a slow flypast with everything down.**

Saunders-Roe

Saunders-Roe, often abbreviated to Saro, was established in 1929 when Alliott Verdon Roe departed from the Avro organisation and joined up with S. E. Saunders Ltd on the Isle of Wight. The firm was based at East Cowes on the River Medina and prior to the Second World War continued to build water-based aircraft. This went on to include the not very successful Lerwick military flying boat of 1938 and, postwar, the phenomenal Princess passenger boat flown in 1952. Also established during the war was a facility at Beaumaris on Anglesey which from 1945 concentrated on small ships and boats. Saro Beaumaris also worked in collaboration with Short Brothers on the wing of the Shetland flying boat described below, with Shorts handling the fuselage. For a period during the 1950s Saunders-Roe became involved in the design of jet- and rocket-powered fighters while an earlier product was the SR.A/1 flying boat fighter, this design and the SR.53 representing the whole of Saro's fighter output. During the 1950s Saunders-Roe also moved into the field of helicopters; towards the end of the decade it was heavily involved with hovercraft, and in the same decade it worked on the Black Knight and Black Arrow space rockets. In 1959 the company was taken over by Westland Aircraft and today the famous hangar on the waterside at Cowes still exists as part of the AgustaWestland Group.

Saunders-Roe SR.A/1

Three prototypes of this flying boat jet fighter design were built, the only such example of this category of aircraft to be produced in the UK. Previously there had been a few proposals for conventional piston-powered boat fighters, but jet engines capable of being fitted inside a small flying boat would reduce drag and offer a performance approaching that of a landplane. The first SR.A/1 flew on 16 July 1947 with the others both following during 1948 and all were powered by two Metropolitan-Vickers F.2/4 Beryl axial turbojets. One example attended Farnborough in September 1948 but sadly two were lost in accidents (one of them fatally). In the end there was little chance of any production orders because the type became somewhat outdated against the rapid increases in performance shown by contemporary ground-based fighter designs, some of which were to have supersonic capability. However, the SR.A/1 boat fighter was a remarkable effort and the sole survivor, TG263 with Class B Mark G-12-1, continued flying until June 1951.

Saunders-Roe SR.53

A concept looked at closely during the early 1950s was the rocket fighter to perform high altitude interceptions and in due course two types were ordered in Britain, the Avro 720 (abandoned in 1955

before it was completed) and the Saunders-Roe SR.53. Two examples of Saro's aircraft were built, the first making its maiden flight on 16 May 1957 and the second on 8 December 1957. Powered by an Armstrong Siddeley Viper turbojet and a de Havilland Spectre rocket motor the SR.53 could easily achieve speeds well in excess of Mach 1. However, long before the type had entered flight test it had been recognised that it would not be suitable as a production machine for operational service, and so the much larger SR.177 was ordered (that project was cancelled in 1957). As a whole the SR.53s served as excellent prototype demonstrators for providing experience in rocket power and operation at high altitudes, although the second aircraft was lost in a fatal crash in June 1958. The first example, serial XD145, made its last flight in October 1959.

ABOVE The first of three Saunders-Roe SR.A/1 prototypes TG263 is seen here moored in the River Medina at Saro's home at East Cowes on the Isle of Wight. *Aeroplane*

LEFT Two detail views of the Saunders-Roe SR.53 rocket fighter prototype XD151 showing the aircraft on display at Farnborough in September 1957, when it was still to fly. An Armstrong Siddeley Viper jet was mounted in the upper rear fuselage with a de Havilland Spectre rocket motor underneath. The de Havilland Firestreak air-to-air missiles mounted on the wingtips were dummy rounds. *Peter Berry*

Short Brothers

Again, this firm's pre-1945 reputation was based around flying boats. One of the oldest of British aircraft manufacturers, Short Brothers was formed in 1908 by the three Short brothers (Eustace, Horace and Oswald) and in 1913 it established a 'Seaplane Works' at Rochester on the River Medway. Another facility at Rochester Airport was set up in 1933 to handle land-based aircraft, and in 1936 a further factory was built at Belfast. The latter, however, was half owned by the Harland and Wolff shipyard. Then in 1943 Shorts was nationalised and in due course the company's base was transferred to Belfast. The move was completed by 1948 and the Belfast companies were merged to form Short Brothers and Harland Ltd.

BELOW Short Sunderland Mk 5 SZ565 'NS/A' of No. 201 Squadron photographed most probably in 1945. This aircraft was written off after a fatal crash at RAF Calshot on 16 November 1951. *Aeroplane*

Between 1939 and 1945 the company's production efforts were concentrated on the Stirling bomber and Sunderland flying boat. The wartime Stirling did not last long enough after 1945 to find a place in here (some civilian Stirling variants did fly postwar) and Shorts' post-1945 products were quite diverse with civil and military designs and subcontracts to build other manufacturers' aircraft. Nevertheless, Shorts produced quite a number of production and prototype designs and, following the end of the flying-boat era, became involved in a series of pioneering research aircraft. Then came the lightweight short-haul Skyvan of 1963 and the Belfast heavy transport of 1964. In 1989 Shorts was bought by the Canadian firm Bombardier, by which time it was building the Tucano trainer for the RAF, and today the Belfast factory is still active building aircraft parts. The Rochester factory was closed in 1948.

Short Sunderland

One of the success stories of the Second World War, the Sunderland also went on to complete a long and successful postwar career. First flown in October 1937 the flying boat was built in five versions and the final GR.Mk 5 variant was powered by four Pratt & Whitney R1830 Twin Wasp engines. After 1945 RAF Sunderlands in the European region took part in the Berlin Air Lift of 1948 but they proved most valuable in the Far East where well-developed runways were still not available in any numbers. RAF squadrons operated them in the Singapore area until 1959 with some units taking a role in the Korean War, and the French Air Force kept Sunderlands until 1962 and the Royal New Zealand Air Force operated examples until 1967. The Mk IV Sunderland was in fact a more heavily modified aircraft and was eventually renamed the Seaford. This type saw brief service after 1945 but some civil conversions of both Sunderland and Seaford, known respectively as the Sandringham and Solent, lasted into the 1950s.

Short Shetland

The Shetland was the last large flying boat to come out of Short Brothers and the first prototype DX166 made its maiden flight on 14 December 1944. It was fitted with four Bristol Centaurus radial engines but was destroyed by fire in January 1946. The second prototype DX171 was converted for civil use with passenger seating as the Shetland II and flew on 17 September 1947. It was scrapped in 1951.

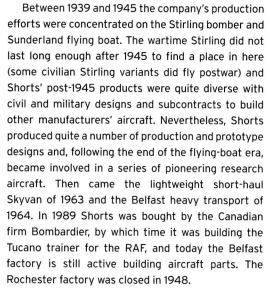

LEFT New Zealand Sunderland NZ4107 pictured in 1967. This aircraft, formerly RAF VB883 transferred in 1952, flew the last official Sunderland flight by the Royal New Zealand Air Force on 2 April 1967 and was scrapped in August of that year.

Short Sturgeon and S.B.3

The first of two prototype Sturgeon torpedo bombers flew on 7 June 1946 powered by a pair of Rolls-Royce Merlins but the type did not enter production; the second prototype flew until the end of 1949. However, a modified target tug version with an extended nose, first flown on 18 May 1948, did achieve a small production run and joined the Fleet Air Arm. In due course many were retrofitted with a smaller nose and the Sturgeon tugs were finally withdrawn in 1958. Charles Brown took some colour of the torpedo bomber prototype, but no colour images have been found for a tug aircraft. There were also the two prototypes of the S.B.3 anti-submarine development with a bulbous nose and two Armstrong Siddeley Mamba turboprops. Only one flew, from 12 August 1950 until mid-1951.

Short S.B.4 Sherpa

The Sherpa first flew on 14 July 1951 as the S.B.1 glider and was designed to test the aero-isoclinic wing at low speeds, a new concept using all-moving wingtips to deal with aeroelasticity – the upward bending or flexing of the outer wing under air load which gave a loss of incidence at the tips. After an accident the glider was rebuilt and fitted with two small Blackburn Turbomeca Palas jets, flying again on 4 October 1953 as the S.B.4 Sherpa. Its flying programme continued into the 1960s and a high speed research aircraft was also planned, but that was never built.

ABOVE Gorgeous photograph of the Short Shetland prototype DX166 which was almost certainly taken on 31 May 1945. This aircraft survived for just over a year before being destroyed by fire on 28 January 1946. *Aeroplane*

LEFT No colour has been traced for the S.B.4 Sherpa research aircraft which was built to test the aero-isoclinic wing at low speeds. *Shorts*

LEFT **LEFT** The second Short Sperrin prototype VX161 pictured at the RAE Golden Jubilee celebrations at Farnborough in early July 1955. The aircraft was parked on the compass-base near 'A' Shed and, with bomb bay doors open, was shown ready to receive a 10,000lb (4,536kg) folding fin bomb placed on the ground underneath. *Peter Berry*

Short S.A.4 Sperrin

The only jet bomber design to be flown by Shorts, the Sperrin was never to progress beyond prototype status once the aerodynamically more advanced V-Bombers had proved themselves. The first Sperrin (VX158) flew on 10 August 1951 powered by four Rolls-Royce Avon jets mounted in wing nacelles (the type was named Sperrin in 1954). The second flew in 1952 and, as a trial, VX158 eventually had the Avons in the lower part of each nacelle replaced by more powerful de Havilland Gyron turbojets. Both machines were successfully employed on research and continued flying until the second half of the 1950s.

Short S.B.5

The one-off S.B.5 was built as a 7/8th linear scale model of the English Electric P.1 research aircraft (Chapter Three) to test that aircraft's highly swept wings and tail position at low speeds. The RAE had serious concerns in regard to the choice of the P.1's low tail position and the S.B.5 could be fitted with alternative 'T' and low tails. It could also have its wing sweep adjusted to angles of 50°, 60° and 69°, although any changes were made on the ground – in flight the wing was fixed. A first flight was achieved on 2 December 1952 and, once the P.1's low tail had been

ABOVE By the time of the Farnborough Show of September 1955 the first Sperrin VX158 had been fitted with de Havilland Gyron jets in the lower position of each engine nacelle. The larger diameter and more powerful Gyron required the lower nacelle section to be widened. *Peter Berry*

RIGHT The Short S.B.5 low speed research aircraft WG768 photographed on the runway during the Farnborough Air Show in September 1953. *Peter Green*

cleared, the S.B.5 was used for general research including some low speed tests for the Concorde supersonic airliner. After several years of service with the Empire Test Pilots' School at Farnborough, the S.B.5's flying career was brought to an end in 1967.

Short S.B.6 Seamew

A lightweight naval anti-submarine aircraft for the RAF and Navy, the first of three Seamew prototypes flew on 23 August 1953. It was designed to be cheaper and relatively simple to operate and maintain compared to the more sophisticated Fairey Gannet (Chapter Three) and thus to appeal to more export customers. Despite showing some poor handling characteristics the Seamew's carrier trials were completed in 1955 aboard HMS *Bulwark*. A total of twenty-four production Seamews were flown before the project was cancelled in 1957.

Short S.C.1

Apart from the Hawker P.1127 and Kestrel discussed in Chapter Three, the only other jet-powered fixed wing vertical take-off aircraft to be test flown in the UK was the Short S.C.1. In fact the S.C.1 was the first jet-powered vertical take-off aircraft to be capable also of forward flight. Britain's first jet-powered 'aircraft' capable of making a vertical take-off and landing had been the Rolls-Royce 'Flying Bedstead' of 1953 which proved that jet lift and control was satisfactory for the vertical flight phase. The S.C.1 took the research on to investigating the transition from vertical to horizontal flight and the first of two examples built made a first conventional flight on 2 April 1957. The first double transitions (vertical take-off to forward flight and then stop to make a vertical landing) were completed on 6 April 1960, the first time this had been achieved by a jet-powered fixed-wing aircraft anywhere in the world. Despite the second aircraft suffering a fatal crash in 1963, the two S.C.1s continued their test flying programmes until 1968 (first) and the early 1970s (second) respectively.

RIGHT TOP Two examples of the Short Seamew light anti-submarine aircraft fly in formation in the mid-1950s. Nearest and painted in naval colours is prototype XA213 and behind, unpainted, most probably the first prototype XA209. *Shorts*

RIGHT CENTRE AND BOTTOM XG900 was the first Short S.C.1 prototype vertical take-off research aircraft to be completed and is seen here on 'away from base' trials to assess the value of the VTOL concept for future operations. These trials were conducted by RAE Bedford. *Clive Rustin*

Supermarine

Supermarine was a company which during the 1920s and 1930s was building flying boats and seaplanes, most spectacularly of course the Schneider Trophy racing seaplanes up until 1931. It was the Spitfire which switched the emphasis to fighters and that aircraft needs no introduction. Its wartime success was spectacular and together with the naval Seafire brought huge production runs. The name Supermarine first appeared in 1916 as the Supermarine Aviation Works Ltd, on the renaming of Pemberton-Billing Ltd situated on the banks of the River Itchen at Woolston in Southampton. By 1940 a new factory had been built at Itchen but bombing raids took production work away to 'dispersed' sites in southern England. Woolston never again produced complete aircraft and the factory had closed by the end of the 1940s.

The design and development organisation was moved to Hursley Park, a mansion near Winchester, and stayed there until 1957. In 1938 Supermarine came under the Vickers-Armstrong umbrella as that organisation's Supermarine Division and in

1960 automatically went into the British Aircraft Corporation. In 1945 Vickers acquired a factory at South Marston near Swindon (which had been built as a shadow factory in 1940) and this became the main Supermarine facility (with its own airfield) until the end of Supermarine fighter production in 1961. From 1947 until 1957 Chilbolton airfield in Hampshire served as Supermarine's flight test centre for jet fighter prototypes and development aircraft, the firm having moved there from its earlier flight test base at High Post. Apart from the postwar prototype Seagull flying boat first flown in July 1948, Supermarine's postwar efforts concentrated entirely on fighter types.

Supermarine Spitfire and Seafire

The Spitfire first flew in March 1936 and versions powered by the Rolls-Royce Griffon were still in production as late as 1948. A great number of Spitfires were assembled by the Castle Bromwich shadow factory near Birmingham which was built in 1938/39, with flight testing at nearby Castle Bromwich aerodrome (after the war this factory switched to car manufacture). Spitfires in the Far East were used against terrorists in Indonesia and Malaya and numerous Royal Auxiliary Air Force squadrons flew examples in the UK, before the Spitfire was finally retired from RAF service in 1955. The final mark of Seafire, the F.Mk 47 again with the Griffon, was manufactured until January 1949. Fleet Air Arm Seafires also took part in attacks over Malaya and became involved in the Korean War, before the type was withdrawn in 1950 from frontline units. Royal Navy Volunteer Reserve Squadrons kept Mk 47 Seafires until 1954.

Supermarine Spiteful and Seafang

The final design in the Spitfire/Seafire line, the Griffon-powered Spiteful and its Seafang naval version, replaced the Spitfire's elliptical wing with a straight tapered laminar flow wing. A modified Spitfire airframe with the new wing flew in June 1944 and the first true Spiteful prototype began flight testing on 8 January 1945. The first Seafang flew in 1946 but orders for both types were cancelled, in part through the rapid progress made in jet fighters. Seafang flying had ceased by around the end of 1949 while the Spiteful's flying career had closed some time earlier.

Supermarine Attacker

The Attacker jet fighter was originally begun as the Jet Spiteful with a Spiteful type wing joined to a special fuselage housing a Rolls-Royce Nene jet engine. The first of three non-naval Supermarine 392 prototypes first flew on 27 July 1946 but the

project was turned down by the RAF. A naval version called the Attacker entered service in 1951 and eventually equipped three frontline squadrons, and some examples were also bought by Pakistan. This was the Royal Navy's first jet fighter but, overall, it was an ordinary design handicapped in part through having a tailwheel undercarriage. However, in its relatively brief career the Attacker provided the Navy with valuable experience in the operation of jet aircraft, in readiness for the types that followed.

Supermarine Types 510 and 535

The Type 510 research aircraft was basically an Attacker fitted with a swept wing. Two examples were built and the first (VV106) became airborne on 29 December

ABOVE Supermarine Seafire F.Mk 47 VR961 '166/CW' of No. 759 Squadron was employed as a 'run around' when it was captured at Ford in November 1953. *Don Clayton via Peter Dance/Air Britain*

LEFT The Attacker was Supermarine's first jet fighter. This rare colour view shows WK320 '833', an FB.Mk 2 belonging to No. 1833 Squadron of the Royal Naval Volunteer Reserve. It was taken in about 1956 at RAF Honiley. *A E Hughes via the late Ray Sturtivant/Air Britain*

BELOW The Attacker/510/535 line ended with the RAF's Swift. WK205 shown here was a Swift F.Mk. 1 which eventually joined No. 56 Squadron in October 1954, although this image was made in mid-February 1954 during a delivery flight from Supermarine's South Marston works to West Raynham. *MoD Crown Copyright*

ABOVE The Supermarine 510 was a swept-wing version of the Attacker and the upper view shows the first 510 VV106. The lower image shows the second aircraft VV119 after it had been heavily modified to become the Type 535.

1948. The 510 retained the tailwheel but in 1950 VV106 achieved deck landings and take-offs on the carrier HMS *Illustrious*, the first swept-wing aircraft to do this. The first 510 continued flying until 1954 to complete a successful programme. In the meantime the second (VV119) had flown in March 1950, but almost immediately it was rebuilt with a tricycle undercarriage and a lengthened nose and fitted with an afterburning version of the Nene to become the Type 535. It made a second maiden flight on 23 August 1950 and as such provided the basis for the Swift. VV119 also had

a successful research career before its retirement in 1955, and it starred in the feature film *The Sound Barrier*. No colour photo was available to the author of either airframe but the issue of *Flight* magazine for 31 October 1981 includes a lovely picture of VV106.

Supermarine Swift

Following on from the 510/535 series Supermarine produced the Type 541 which became the prototype for the Swift. The 541 brought many changes including an Avon axial jet and the first example flew on 1 August

RIGHT A Swift FR.Mk 5 of 79 Squadron, XD953 'R', is seen on display at an air show in the UK (probably Cottesmore) in 1957. A Gloster Javelin is parked behind.
Graham Hopkin

LEFT WK273 was an F. Mk 4 fighter version of the Supermarine Swift and in September 1954 was displayed at the Farnborough Air Show with underwing rocket projectiles or bombs. This aircraft spent its entire career on company trials and development programmes before its retirement in 1959.

LEFT The Swift F.Mk 7 featured a longer nose and could carry the Fairey Fireflash air-to-air missile. Only fourteen were built and this view shows one, thought to be XF123, at RAF Valley in 1957/58 while serving with No. 1 Guided Weapons Development Squadron. *Alan Curry*

1951. The second prototype brought even more alterations including a more forward cockpit and extended air intakes and flew on 14 July 1952. Deliveries to an RAF squadron (No. 56) began in 1954 but Supermarine's last RAF fighter struggled in its intended interceptor role and spent just over a year with this unit. Its flying capabilities at altitude were poor, but in the low-level short-range fighter reconnaissance role the later FR.Mk 5 version served successfully with two squadrons in RAF Germany during the second half of the 1950s. The Swift was retired in 1961.

Supermarine Types 508 and 529

Running alongside the 510/Swift series for the RAF came another for a larger heavy fighter for the Navy. Three examples of the near straight wing Type 508 fitted with a V-tail were ordered and the first, VX133, entered flight test on 31 August 1951; the second (VX136 slightly modified as the Type 529) followed almost a year later. Two Avons were installed and the first airframe completed a long flying programme, although VX136 experienced a much shorter career after it had suffered extensive damage from a landing accident in December 1953.

LEFT The Supermarine 508 heavy fighter featured a very distinctive V-tail. VX133 is pictured here at RAE Bedford in July 1957 where it had been used for arrestor gear development. *Peter Berry*

RIGHT Scimitars were eventually equipped to carry the American Sidewinder air-to-air missile and XD239 '613' of No. 736 Squadron Royal Navy is shown in 1962 carrying dummy training rounds under each wing.

Supermarine 525

To reflect advances in high speed aerodynamics the third Type 508 prototype was fitted with a swept wing plus a conventional tailplane and fin as the Type 525, and as such first flew on 27 April 1954. In this form it served in many respects as a prototype for the Scimitar below and continued flying until it crashed in July 1955. The sole Type 525, VX138, also attended the 1954 Farnborough Air Show.

Supermarine Scimitar

The heavy Scimitar day fighter was the last Supermarine fighter. The first of three Type 544 prototypes, still powered by a pair of Avons, flew on 19 January 1956 and the type entered service in 1957. It went on to equip four frontline squadrons and operated initially as a fighter, but the arrival of de Havilland's Sea Vixen (Chapter Two) to take most of the Navy's interception duties left the Scimitar to operate in the conventional and nuclear strike role. Supermarine's aircraft was also used as an in-flight refuelling tanker (with operations on the Beira Patrol in 1966) and the type was finally retired from the front line in 1966. However, Airwork Fleet Requirements Unit used the Scimitar for training until late 1970.

ABOVE The one-off Type 525 VX138 introduced a swept wing and tailplane and dispensed with the V-tail. It is shown here at the 1954 Farnborough Show. *Don Clayton via Peter Dance/Air Britain*

RIGHT XD268 '156/V' was a Scimitar belonging to No. 803 Squadron and is seen here lined up on the Farnborough runway about to display in the 1960 SBAC Show. Underwing pylons are in place but are not in use. This aircraft was lost in a crash on 15 July 1965.

XD236 '038' was serving with Airwork Fleet
Requirements Unit when it was pictured flying off the
Isle of Wight in the spring or early summer of 1968. On
26 June 1968, soon after this image was made, XD236
flew into high ground on the Isle of Wight.

Vickers-Armstrong

ABOVE TOP The second Vickers Valiant prototype WB215 is seen about to touch down at Farnborough. The silver colour scheme was eventually replaced on production machines by an all-white livery.

ABOVE Making a good comparison to the picture of WB215, here we see a production Valiant XD817 of No. 148 Squadron coming into land at Farnborough on 7 September 1960. Although not of perfect quality this shot does show some of the modifications made to series aircraft.
Terry Panopalis

Unlike many British aircraft manufacturers who began under the control of one or more individuals, Vickers entered the field of aircraft construction as a long-established heavy engineering firm. Vickers was formed as a steel manufacturer in 1828 and established an aviation division in 1911, providing fighters and bombers during the First World War and the 1920s and 1930s. A peak was reached with the splendid Wellington bomber that achieved so much during the early years of the Second World War. In 1927 Vickers merged with Sir W.G. Armstrong Whitworth to form Vickers-Armstrong. A year later the Aviation Department was renamed Vickers (Aviation) Ltd and the acquisition of Supermarine shortly afterwards resulted in the title Supermarine Aviation Works (Vickers) Ltd for that branch of the organisation. Ten years later they became Vickers-Armstrongs (Aircraft) Ltd but kept their Vickers and Supermarine identities as separate Divisions. In 1960 Vickers-Armstrongs (Aircraft) became a major part of BAC. Alongside its aircraft business, during the 1940s and 1950s the company entered the fields of bomb and guided missile development.

Vickers' main factory was based at Brooklands near Weybridge south of London. For many years new experimental aircraft, right up to the Valiant jet bomber prototypes, were built by the experimental department at Foxwarren, a hangar situated between Weybridge and Wisley. For the war effort Vickers also had a large shadow factory built at Chester (Hawarden) which in 1948 passed to de Havilland control. Due to the size of the Brooklands field, after the war newly completed aircraft would be flown from there to another airfield at Wisley to complete their testing. Wisley, a little to the south, had opened in 1944. The Wellington was followed on the production line by the Warwick and both types saw some postwar service, but the Windsor bomber and Type 432 fighter prototypes had completed their flying careers by 1946 and 1944 respectively, in the process avoiding the colour camera. A long postwar series of airliners – the Valetta, Varsity, Viscount, Vanguard and the jet powered VC-10 (the latter continued by BAC) – complemented the Valiant jet bomber programme. The airfield at Wisley was closed in 1973 and the factory at Brooklands in 1988.

Vickers Warwick

The first Vickers Warwick bomber flew in August 1939 but few were delivered as bombers before production was switched to transport and air/sea rescue versions. The final variant was the GR.Mk V anti-submarine and general reconnaissance aircraft. When the war ended, a number of squadrons were still equipped with different Warwick versions but all had been retired by the end of 1946.

Vickers Valiant

The Vickers Valiant B.Mk 1 was the first V-Bomber to fly and the three types (Avro Vulcan, Handley Page Victor and the Valiant) were responsible for the delivery of Britain's strategic nuclear deterrent from the mid-1950s, when the Valiant entered service, through to 1969 when the submarine-launched Polaris took over. It was the Valiant which performed the first trial drops of Britain's nuclear bombs. However, the type was also used as a conventional bomber (in 1956 some aircraft took part in the Suez Crisis), as a strategic photo-reconnaissance aircraft and later as a tactical bomber and an in-flight refuelling tanker. The Mk.1 was withdrawn and scrapped prematurely in 1965 after fatigue cracks had been discovered in the main spars of many aircraft, although one airframe fitted with a new spar did continue flying until 1968.

Only one example of the B.Mk 2 low level 'Pathfinder' Valiant was built, WJ954, which famously was painted in an all-black colour scheme and attended the Farnborough Air Show in September 1954.

ABOVE Early in their careers the V-Bombers were finished in a silver colour scheme, including Vickers Valiant XD826 seen here at Wethersfield in the summer of 1957. *Mike Hooks*

LEFT Valiant BK.Mk 1 XD815 pictured at Cottesmore in 1957. At the time the aircraft was serving with No. 148 Squadron. *Graham Hopkin*

ABOVE It is sometimes forgotten what a graceful aeroplane the Vickers Valiant was, but hopefully this view will serve as a reminder. It shows XD816 which was the only example to be fitted with new wing spars. As a result, after the discovery of wing fatigue problems had seen the Valiant withdrawn from RAF service in early 1965, XD816 continued flying for several years on a Ministry trials programme looking into metal fatigue. It is pictured here in May 1967 performing a flypast prior to landing at Wisley.

FACING PAGE TOP Another view of XD816, this time performing a flyover at Scampton during the event that marked the disbanding of Bomber Command on 29 April 1968 to be replaced by Strike Command. A Vulcan, a Victor and the Valiant all flew over as the ensign was lowered. *Terry Panopalis*

FACING PAGE BOTTOM The 'Black Bomber'. The sole Vickers Valiant B.Mk 2 WJ954 is seen on the runway at Farnborough during the SBAC Show of 1954. *Mike Hooks*

Westland

Although well known today for its achievements in helicopter design and manufacture, Westland had a long run with fixed wing aeroplanes before moving into the field of rotary wings. The factory at Yeovil was established in 1915 and is still operating today, but Westland Aircraft Ltd was not formed until 1935 – prior to that date the manufacturer had been part of Petters Ltd, a petrol and diesel engine company. The most famous wartime products were the Whirlwind fighter and Lysander army co-operation aircraft – the Welkin high altitude fighter of 1942 entered production but did not enter service. A Whirlwind and the odd Welkin (including the sole example of the Welkin Mk II) flew in the immediate postwar years, but the only Westland fixed wing type to achieve production and service after 1945 was the Wyvern. After acquiring a licensing agreement with the American firm Sikorsky, Westland went on to specialise in helicopters. A merger of Fairey's aviation interests with Westland took place in early 1960, which came shortly after Westland had acquired the Saunders-Roe group and the helicopter division of Bristol. In

1961 the resulting company was called Westland Helicopters and it took on all UK helicopter work, BAC and HSA concentrating on fixed wing aircraft. Consequently, Westland was not affected by the 1977 nationalisation of the two giants into British Aerospace, but in 2000 it did merge with the Italian helicopter outfit Agusta to form AgustaWestland.

Westland Wyvern

A large chunky naval strike fighter, the Wyvern was the world's first and only turboprop attack aircraft to enter squadron service. The first prototype made its maiden flight on 12 December 1946 with a Rolls-Royce Eagle piston engine and other examples flew with an Armstrong Siddeley Python or a Rolls-Royce Clyde turboprop (the Python was subsequently chosen for the production run). However, the aircraft experienced a difficult development programme and suffered several crashes. Wyverns first joined the Fleet Air Arm in 1953 but the aircraft was not particularly successful. The ultimate version was the TF.Mk 4 (later retitled S. Mk 4) and the last examples were retired in 1958.

ABOVE AND FACING PAGE
The Westland Wyvern was a very impressive-looking naval strike aircraft. Two S.Mk 4s are pictured here at RNAS Ford in November 1953. They are VZ752 '182' and VZ753 '183', both of which belonged to No. 813 Squadron based at the time at Ford.
Don Clayton via Peter Dance/Air Britain

Chapter Five

Air Shows, Government Establishments and Testing

The background to the British Aircraft Industry is not just a case of listing and describing the various manufacturers and design teams involved and the aircraft that they produced. A hugely important element was the Government establishments that provided research, back-up support and a lot of additional facilities for testing. These covered everything from basic research into aerodynamics, materials, electronics, fuels and so on, to the wind tunnel testing of proposed shapes, the stress testing of full size airframes and the flight testing of the finished aeroplane. This is not the place to provide an exhaustive list of all of the Government establishments that were involved with aviation, but this chapter does take a look at the most important - in effect the key players and in particular those which feature in many of the photographs presented in these pages. Essentially, this means the Aeroplane & Armament Experimental Establishment (A&AEE) at Boscombe Down and the Royal Aircraft Establishment (RAE) at Farnborough and Bedford. RAE also had facilities for example at Llanbedr in Wales and there were other important operators of military aircraft types such as the Royal Radar Establishment (RRE) at Malvern and Pershore. Back in 1945 RRE was called the Telecommunications Research Establishment (TRE) but in 1953 its name was changed to the Radar Research Establishment, and in 1957 to Royal Radar Establishment. The author mentions TRE/RRE here simply to show that just keeping track of the names can be difficult (today this organisation still exists as part of Qinetiq).

ABOVE XA552 was a Gloster Javelin FAW.Mk 1 which spent most of its flying career on trials work. This lovely picture was taken by Russell Adams in the mid-1950s. In due course it was fitted with two de Havilland Gyron Junior engines to serve as a test bed for the Bristol 188's powerplant (Chapter Two). For that purpose it was painted in a royal blue finish. *Jet Age Museum*

All of the firms listed in the previous chapters were members of the Society of British Aircraft Constructors or SBAC (which later became the Society of British Aerospace Companies). This body was the UK aircraft industry's national trade association and represented companies supplying all manner of aircraft and equipment to aviation customers, in the civil, military and space sectors; indeed almost every aircraft and engine manufacturer, and related firms such as metal alloy suppliers, would join the SBAC. This body was of course behind the Farnborough trade and business shows which feature so strongly in this volume. These trade events were first held by the SBAC in the 1930s and the first postwar gatherings took place in September 1946 and September 1947 at Radlett. In 1948 this annual occasion in September moved to Farnborough where it has been based ever since. As a shop window for new products they were also some of the few occasions where (from 1948) the public could see what were normally very secret aeroplanes. From 1962 it went biennial and more recently the Show has been held in July. In 2009 the SBAC was merged with two other bodies (including the Defence Manufacturers' Association) to form the ADS Group.

Aeroplane and Armament Experimental Establishment, Boscombe Down

A&AEE at Boscombe Down near Salisbury in Wiltshire was opened in 1939 after the organisation had moved from its previous home at Martlesham

Heath on the east coast of England. Boscombe was (and still is) the facility where new British military aircraft were checked and cleared for service use, and it also witnessed the first flights of many British prototype aircraft. An important reason why so many types of aeroplane started their flying careers at Boscombe, rather than at the factories where they had been built, was the Establishment's long runway, which made it an ideal location for such important events. In 1992 the A&AEE became part of the Defence Research Agency (DRA), during the following year the control of the Boscombe Down facility came under the Defence Test and Evaluation Organisation (DTEO), and in 1995 this control passed to the Defence Evaluation and Research Agency or DERA. In 2001 DERA was split into two parts, one section going to the civil service Defence Science and Technology Laboratory (DSTL), the other to form part of the private company known as Qinetiq.

The Royal Aircraft Establishment at Farnborough

Farnborough, like Hendon and Brooklands, is one of the great names of British aviation and indeed did much to bring the British aviation industry into existence. What was started in 1908 as HM Balloon Factory became in 1911 the Royal Aircraft Factory. During the First World War the factory produced many aircraft but in 1918 it was renamed to prevent any confusion with the newly formed Royal Air Force. The new title was the Royal Aircraft

BELOW This splendid view of the SBAC Show at Farnborough in 1955 shows a remarkable range of aeroplanes, all of which came from UK industry. At the front running clockwise from left we have a Fairey Gannet, Avro Vulcan XA890, the de Havilland Comet jet airliner, the four-engine Handley Page HPR.3 Herald airliner prototype, Handley Page Victor prototype, two-seat Hawker Hunter prototype XJ615, two single-seat Hunters – WV385 (rear) and WW593 (at the front), Folland Gnat G-39-2, Fairey Delta II and a Gloster Javelin. The far background has the Avro Ashton flying laboratory, Avro Shackleton WR970, the Short Sperrin with Gyron engine in the lower port nacelle only and the Napier Eland Airspeed Ambassador test bed, while in front of the aircraft are a range of road vehicles to delight the modeller. Oh to be able to step into this photo and take a look at so many different aircraft! *Aeroplane*

Establishment and in due course the organisation moved on to performing all manner of general aviation research, for which an immensely impressive collection of testing facilities (including wind tunnels) was gradually assembled. Some of the most important research in aviation history has been performed at the various RAE sites, and particularly so at Farnborough.

In 1988 the wording for RAE was changed to the Royal Aerospace Establishment and in April 1991 it was merged into the DRA, the new title for the MoD's research organisation. In April 1995 the DRA and other MoD establishments were merged into DERA and, as explained above, in 2001 DERA was split into DSTL and Qinetiq. Today many of the Farnborough research facilities are gone, although important aviation work is still undertaken by Qinetiq and DSTL and other bodies on the site (for example the Air Accidents Investigation Branch). A new Farnborough Aerospace Centre was built between 1990 and 1992 and most of its buildings now serve as the headquarters for BAE Systems.

The Royal Aircraft Establishment at Bedford

In 1946 work began to convert the RAF airfield at Thurleigh into RAE Bedford. This became an important research and experiment facility and was

used for a great deal of aircraft development test flying. During the 1950s and 1960s many of the prototype and experimental aircraft seen within these pages operated with RAE's Aero flights (Aerodynamics Research Flights) flying out of both Bedford and Farnborough. The Bedford airfield was closed in 1997 after its aircraft had been moved to Boscombe Down in 1994 (the flight test fleet at Farnborough was also moved to Boscombe in 1994). Qinetiq sold the last of its share in the Bedford complex in 2008.

Central Fighter Establishment at West Raynham

For over twenty years the Central Fighter Establishment (CFE) was an important element in preparing fighter aircraft for the front line. The objective behind this organisation, which belonged to the RAF, was to test new fighters and their equipment (often against other fighter types and/or other aircraft), the development of fighter aircraft tactics, and to train squadron and flight commanders. It was formed in 1944 and in October 1945 moved to West Raynham, where it stayed until December 1962 when a further move was made to Binbrook. CFE was disbanded on 1 February 1966. This organisation was just one of many training and trials units which operated within the control of the RAF during the period covered by this book.

Aerobatic teams have always been a key element for air show displays all over the country and these images show some of the famous teams from the 1950s and 1960s.

BELOW In 1957 the Royal Navy Sea Hawks of No. 738 Squadron formed a five-ship team with the aircraft painted pillar-box red. This view shows the team landing together after a display at Farnborough in September 1957. *Peter Berry*

ABOVE After the *Red Arrows* of today with their Hawk training aircraft, perhaps the most famous UK display team was the *Black Arrows* of No. 111 Squadron flying Hawker Hunter fighters. The aircraft were painted black and in 1958 the team (joined by Hunters from other squadrons) set a world record when it looped 22 aircraft in formation. *Clive Rustin*

In 1963 No. 56 Squadron formed a nine-aircraft display team with its English Electric Lightnings, which it called the *Firebirds*. Unfortunately this did not include an appearance at Farnborough because 1963 was a blank year, the first after the trade show had gone biennial. This view shows the *Firebirds* in practice.

FACING PAGE TOP English Electric Canberra B.Mk 2 WD952 is seen under tow at the 1955 Farnborough being taken from the static display area to be made ready for its flying display. This aircraft had been fitted experimentally with a pair of Olympus turbojets as a test bed, replacing the Canberra's usual Avons, and with this powerplant it twice broke the world altitude record. A Scottish Aviation Twin Pioneer is being towed in the background. *Peter Berry*

FACING PAGE BOTTOM Gloster Javelin F(AW). Mk 1 XA552 was from 1961 used to flight test the de Havilland Gyron Junior DGJ.10 in readiness for this engine to be used in the Bristol 188 research aircraft. The dark blue finish with red lettering and the redesigned jetpipes resulted in what might be considered to be the most attractive of all Javelins. *Terry Panopalis*

ABOVE Handley Page Victor B.Mk 1 XH588 took part in the 1960 Farnborough Show. *Peter Green*

ABOVE AND RIGHT Two photographs showing the RAE Aero Flight line at Bedford on the same day in 1962. The first shows left to right English Electric P.1 WG763, Short S.B.5 WG768, Avro 707A WZ736 and the Handley Page HP.115 XP841 (with the engine cover removed). The second shot taken a little later has the HP.115 replaced by a Meteor night fighter, and a Royal Navy Westland Whirlwind helicopter has joined the line. At this time the P.1 was no longer flying, but was being used for arrestor trials. *Clive Rustin*

FACING PAGE Not the best quality but these images are included because they are rare - in fact quite unique! Featuring an unidentified Hawker Tempest II they were taken at Farnborough in late July or early August 1945 by Bell Aircraft test pilot Jack Woolams, who was on a visit to RAE from America. Tragically, Woolams died just over a year later on 30 August 1946 when the high speed Bell P-39 Airacobra he was flying crashed into Lake Ontario. *Mrs J. Woolams via Phil Butler*

RIGHT The Handley Page HP.115 flying over the English Channel in June 1965 on its journey to the Paris Air Show. This aircraft was part of RAE Bedford's Aero Flight, which is indicated by the markings on its nose. *Clive Rustin*

ABOVE, LEFT AND FACING PAGE TOP On 18 June 1966 the last Hawker P.1127 prototype research aircraft XP984 performed a series of vertical take-off and landing trials aboard the carrier HMS *Bulwark*. *Clive Rustin*

FACING PAGE BOTTOM The very first P.1127 XP831 continued research flying well into the 1970s and is seen here flying over Aylesbury in 1971 when still in the hands of RAE Bedford's Aerodynamics Flight. It was withdrawn from use in 1972. Strictly speaking this image falls outside the book's parameters, but in fact the P.1127 was very much an aircraft of the 1960s and photos of XP831 flying late in its career appear to be quite rare. *Adrian Balch*

LEFT This set of pictures shows two early Blackburn Buccaneers, development aircraft XK489 with a nose probe and 'Buccaneer' painted on its nose and S.Mk 1 XK527 with a yellow nose, carrying out deck trials aboard the carrier HMS *Ark Royal* in mid-November 1960. *Dennis Higton*

FACING PAGE TOP Another Buccaneer, the first production S.Mk 1 XK523, performed some deck trials aboard HMS *Victorious* during the first months of 1960. *Dennis Higton*

FACING PAGE BOTTOM Buccaneer S. Mk 1 XN923 photographed aboard HMS *Ark Royal* in the English Channel in 1964 while undergoing trials with some new equipment. These were to do with inertial trials in aircraft and looking at the transfer of data from ship to aircraft. The pilot was Lt. Brian Bullivant. The new S. Mk 2 Buccaneer variant with Rolls-Royce Spey engines was performing its deck trials at the same time. *David Eagles*

Pictures showing Hawker Hunters operating with the Empire Test Pilots' School (ETPS), which during the 1960s was based at RAE Farnborough.

ABOVE Empire Test Pilots' School Hawker Hunter F.Mk 4 XF969 '26' at Gaydon on 14 September 1963. Note the red nose probe. *The late Roff Jones*

LEFT Two-seat Hunter T.Mk 7A WV253 '24', probably photographed at Boscombe Down. On 15 July 1968 this aircraft crashed into Lyme Bay. *The late Mike Stroud*

FACING PAGE TOP Hawker Hunter F.Mk 6 XG192 'F' at the Cottesmore Air Show in 1957. The yellow spine signifies that this aircraft belonged to the Day Fighter Leaders' School which formed part of CFE at West Raynham. This aircraft was written off in a crash in Cyprus on 16 January 1962. *Graham Hopkin*

FACING PAGE BOTTOM Another Hunter F6, XF382 'R', seen in about 1958. In March 1958 the Day Fighter Leaders' School was redesignated Day Fighter Combat Squadron (DFCS), as part of the Fighter Combat School of CFE still at West Raynham. XF382 is thought to have served as 'R' with the DFCS during 1958, but by the time the picture was taken it may have moved on to No. 229 Operational Conversion Unit as an 'instructor check/bounce' aircraft, specifically for that Unit's flying instructor to 'bounce' new pilots in a practice dogfight. *The late Eric Morgan*

LEFT General view of an RAF Germany air base, quite possibly RAF Ahlhorn in about 1957/58. Hawker Hunters predominate and the hangars are typical Luftwaffe design. *Andy Whitson*

In 1960 No. 700 Squadron, a naval trials unit based at Yeovilton, experimented with Day-Glo paint on parts of some of its Hawker Sea Hawk FGA.Mk 4 jet fighters. WV921 '516 VL' features most prominently in this series of pictures taken in the summer of 1960.
Tony Kilner

LEFT Along with those allocated to experimental and research establishments, and various service training units, many aircraft were used by the manufacturers for their own or customers' trials. In addition, each new aircraft off the production line of course had to have its own clearance tests. This shot shows Gloster Javelin XA649 in the firm's engine test pen. *Jet Age Museum*

ABOVE This Javelin was used by Gloster in the 1950s to trial some anti-spin attachments which can be seen on the tailplane. The aircraft is also towing something, the identity of which remains a mystery. *Jet Age Museum*

RIGHT The author apologises for the profusion of pictures of Gloster Javelins, but this was a very photogenic aircraft. FAW.Mk 2 XA778 pictured at Moreton Valence in late February 1961 was painted entirely in Day-Glo prior to delivery to A&AEE Boscombe Down where it was to serve as a pacer aircraft. In that capacity it was used to help determine airspeed indicator errors on other aircraft. XA778 was scrapped at Boscombe in 1968. *Jet Age Museum*

LEFT AND ABOVE On 19 April 1961 Javelin XH841 was photographed by Russell Adams while being flown by test pilot Don Lucey at an altitude of 50,000ft (15,240m). The deep blue colour of the sky at this altitude is shown beautifully. *Jet Age Museum*

RIGHT One company to use a lot of service aircraft types for all manner of trials programmes was Flight Refuelling Ltd. For example in 1949 a Gloster Meteor F.Mk 3 was fitted with a nose-mounted air-to-air refuelling probe and the aircraft is seen here flying off the south coast of England as it approaches its tanker.
Cobham

BELOW Supermarine Scimitar F.Mk 1 XD229 spent a great deal of its career on trials flying, including Red Beard development work and various other weapons trials with both Supermarine and RAE. Later in its career when serving at RAE West Freugh in 1962 to 1966 it sported a blue and white livery (which is a scheme that is yet to appear in a colour photo). This undated picture was taken before the repaint - note the gold nose and wing and fin leading edges.
Terry Panopalis

ABOVE Many V-Bombers were subsequently converted into in-flight refuelling tankers. These shots show Vickers Valiant XD863 refuelling an English Electric Lightning T.Mk 4 trainer with a white nose.
North West Heritage Group via Joe Cherrie

LEFT In 1963 Rolls-Royce at Hucknall recruited Armstrong Whitworth NF.Mk 14 Meteor WS829 to serve as a photographic chase aircraft using the civil registration G-ASLW. The aeroplane operated in this role until the late 1960s but in November 1969 it was lost off the Cape Verde Islands during a delivery flight to Biafra. *Clive Rustin*

Chapter Six

Press and Industry Photos and Service Views

The primary element of this work has been to present as many good quality colour pictures to readers and enthusiasts as possible. The review of British aircraft manufacturers and the establishments that worked with them has been included really to provide a basic background to how the aeroplanes featured in these pages evolved. The photographic archives of the aircraft firms have been an important source of images but so often they show aeroplanes prior to delivery to the customer, before their service careers had begun. From a modeller's point of view that means the aircraft depicted in manufacturers' images almost always lack squadron and unit markings, which so often gave these machines something of an identity. During the 1950s RAF squadrons in particular had permission to mark their fighters with often quite vivid unit markings (in fact this was one of the most 'colourful' eras in the history of the RAF), so for images of service aircraft we must look at Royal Air Force and Royal Navy archives and, of course, private collections. Camouflage was introduced to day fighters in 1953 to replace the standard overall aluminium silver finish used up to that point, so the variety of colours available to the photographer on RAF aeroplanes was quite something. And of course the Fleet Air Arm provided a further selection.

ABOVE A flight of white Avro Vulcan B.Mk 1s, XA896, XH503 and XH504, belonging to No. 230 Operational Conversion Unit (OCU) pictured in September 1959. Each of these aircraft wears the Waddington station badge. *MoD*

A third and most brilliant source of pictures showing aircraft in service is the aviation press and this final chapter rounds off the book's text with a brief look at the work and careers of certain press and specialist photographers in the 1940s and 1950s. Added to this is some background information on a selection of industry photographers. Perhaps the most famous British aviation photographer for the period we are concerned with, and indeed over the 20th century as a whole, was Charles E. Brown. A freelance photographer, his material has been featured in several books already (as noted in Chapter One) and this collection is now safe and sound in the custody of the RAF Museum at Hendon.

The two main British magazines for reporting the aviation scene during the period 1945 to 1970 was *The Aeroplane* and *Flight*, although from March 1962 the former was renamed *The Aeroplane and Commercial Aviation News*. Both of these publications employed superb masters of the camera but, unfortunately, it has not been possible to credit most of the splendid images made available to the author by today's *Aeroplane* historical magazine to a specific photographer. The collection is held in *Aeroplane*'s archives but there is little in the way of background detail to go with any of the transparencies. During the 1950s the main cameraman for *Flight* was L. W. 'Mac' McLaren, who replaced the famous John Yoxall when the latter left the publication. Yoxall joined the staff of *Flight* in 1913 and did much of his most famous work before the war. However, as early as 1942 he was photographing Mosquitos for *Flight* in colour, and Yoxall colour images were still published in the magazine into the early

1950s. McLaren began to assist Yoxall in about 1929 and over the years assumed an increasing responsibility for air-to-air and general photographic coverage. By the late 1950s Ian Macdonald had joined McLaren and the work of 'the two Macs' became (at the time) as well known as Yoxall's masterpieces.

The Aeroplane photographers Charles Sims and A. E. Long both served with the RAF during the war, which left Maurice Rowe to take photos of new aircraft for the magazine. That meant Rowe was present in the darkroom when colour was first used, but he has told the author that he was pretty sure that *Aeroplane* did not try much colour until Charles Sims experimented with the format in 1945/46. At the time the magazine only had one camera that could handle colour film and, to begin with, the photographers doubted if the new medium would ever be used. Postwar, the job of in-flight photography for *Aeroplane* was gradually taken over by Alf Long, who is remembered for images of some of the famous 1950s and 1960s aerobatic teams. Of course these experts did not just spend their time covering aviation stories - motor racing, for example, would always draw in the best exponents of the camera from other areas like aviation where, one understands, the skill of filming a moving object would have been especially valuable. At an exhibition at the National Gallery in March 1952 Charles Brown was named as one of the three 'Past-Master' aeronautical photographers in the country, along with Charles Sims and John Yoxall.

In regard to photographers working for the aircraft companies, Russell Adams of Gloster was

BELOW Avro Shackleton MR. Mk 2 WR966 seen at Farnborough in July 1955. In the previous March the aircraft had been delivered to the Joint Anti-Submarine School (JASS) Flight as 'G/C', and in March 1957 WR966 joined No. 220 Squadron. *Peter Berry*

one of the best and his work is featured throughout the book. He began taking pictures for the firm in 1949, having joined not as a photographer but as a technical research assistant. He continued to photograph Gloster products, and those from other Hawker Siddeley companies, until 1962 when his employers closed down. Adams very quickly learnt his trade and went on to pioneer jet aerobatic photography, which also reflected his love of flying. He explained his technique of taking photographs of aircraft while they were performing a loop to both Long and Sims. To do this the famous test pilot Jan Żurakowski would fly a two-seat Gloster Meteor T.Mk 7 camera aircraft alongside the subject to be photographed and follow it right through a loop. During the manoeuvre Adams would take his photos, and needless to say the two of them became known as the 'Up and Over Boys'. Adams' story is well told in Tim Kershaw's *Jet Age Photographer* (Sutton 2005) and the author makes no apology for publicising a book which contains a marvellous selection of black and white photographs.

For many years Hawker Aircraft's outstanding photographer was Cyril Peckham who was, perhaps more than most of his photographic colleagues, a great aviation enthusiast. Like Adams, Peckham eventually designed his own camera but in his case the new piece of equipment (which *Flight* described as 'a remarkable weapon') was patented and eventually ordered in quantity for Service use. In due course Peckham became the chief photographer

for the Hawker Siddeley group of aircraft companies. Meanwhile, the wonderful manufacturer's publicity air-to-air views of the Avro Vulcan jet bomber and other Avro products were the work of Paul Cullerne. During the war Cullerne had served with the RAF as a Sergeant Photographer. When he left the Service in 1946 he took up photography for Avro and continued to work for Hawker Siddeley and British Aerospace after the mergers in 1960 and 1977. Leslie Sansom did much the same for Vickers right from the days of open cockpits. All of these photographers would of course supply plenty of their images of new aeroplanes to *The Aeroplane* and *Flight*, and indeed to many other magazines and publications, and not just in the UK but in the United States and France as well. Early Russell Adams pictures for example were used by 198 American publications alone.

Each of these masters did their bit to turn the creation of air-to-air pictures of aeroplanes into an art form. Indeed, aviation has been fortunate that its most famous photographers were essentially artists rather than snapshot men, taking into account the value of cloud and landscapes in their photographs along with sun glint, clear skies and the angles and attitudes of their subjects. Some of the results are quite magnificent and the author is fortunate to have been given the opportunity to use just a selection of images by these experts. But it must not be forgotten that the skills of many of the amateur photographers featured in this book were also quite considerable. They have all contributed so much to the final work.

ABOVE Armstrong Whitworth Meteor NF. Mk 11 WD673 pictured at Blackbushe on 12 October 1957 while in the hands of No. 87 Squadron. This unit was at the time in the process of converting to the Gloster Javelin, a task that was completed in November 1957. *Peter Green*

FACING PAGE ABOVE Avro Vulcan B.Mk 1 XH483 belonged to No. 617 Squadron when it was photographed at Cottesmore in 1959. *Graham Hopkin*

FACING PAGE BELOW Avro Vulcan B.Mk 1 XH499 photographed at Gaydon, probably in the early 1960s. *Terry Panopalis*

LEFT A number of Armstrong Whitworth Meteor Mk 11 night fighters were eventually converted into TT.Mk 20 target tugs for the Royal Navy. This example was spotted at RAF Benson in 1959. Note the Del Mar winch installation mounted above the inner wing. *Peter Green*

BELOW Buccaneer S.Mk 1 XN951 '101/E' of No. 800 Squadron seen on board HMS *Eagle* in 1964/65. This aeroplane was lost in a crash in December 1970 while serving with No. 736 Squadron. *Sir Mark Thomson*

ABOVE This unidentified all-white Blackburn Buccaneer was photographed by Russell Adams as it climbed into a loop. The aircraft shows no unit markings.

Jet Age Museum

LEFT Two de Havilland
F Mk 3 Hornets of No. 80
Squadron captured in
colour flying out of Kai
Tak, Hong Kong, in 1954.
The two aeroplanes are
WB909 'N' nearest and
PX366 'E'. Note the red
and blue propeller hubs.
Peter Green

FACING PAGE Photos
showing de Havilland
Mosquitos from Bomber
Command's Marker
Force receiving first-line
servicing and then
preparing to take off from
their base at Hemswell in
Lincolnshire in the spring
of 1950. The take-off view
includes TK620 'XD/L'
and VP185 'XD/N', both
B.Mk 35s. *Aeroplane*

RIGHT Pictured in early
April 1954 during a visit
by Gloster photographer
Russell Adams to the
carrier HMS *Eagle* is
de Havilland Sea Hornet
NF.Mk 21 VW957 '481/J'
of No. 809 Squadron.
Although the sun is
shining, from the crew's
dress the weather looks
pretty chilly.
Jet Age Museum

LEFT Air-to-air view from late 1955 or very early 1956 of de Havilland Sea Vampire T.Mk 22 '696/FD' from No. 764 Squadron at Ford. This was a holding unit to keep pilots in training before their appointment to a frontline unit. It is understood that the 'badge' on the nose has the three Navy pennant flags for '764'.
David Eagles

BELOW De Havilland Vampire FB.Mk 5 VZ238 '78' of No. 8 Flying Training School (FTS) pictured on a sortie from its base at RAF Swinderby in the summer of 1956.
John Merry

ABOVE A line-up of rather worn de Havilland Venom FB.Mk 1 fighter-bombers start their engines for another day of operations. These were the equipment of No. 145 Squadron based at Celle in West Germany and the picture was taken in 1955/56. The unit acquired the Venom as a replacement for its Vampire fighter-bombers in 1954 and kept the type until it disbanded in October 1957.
Clive Rustin

LEFT A lovely picture of Venom WK418 'G' of No. 145 Squadron in 1955/56, a view which also demonstrates the effectiveness of the camouflage. Note the squadron marking on the outside of the tailboom.
Clive Rustin

LEFT Line-up of de Havilland Sea Venom FAW. Mk 22s from No. 891 Squadron aboard HMS *Bulwark* in 1958. The nearest aircraft is XG730 '438/B' which continued flying until 1970. *Tony Kilner*

BELOW An unidentified Sea Venom Mk 22 is prepared for launching from HMS *Bulwark's* starboard catapult in 1958. *Tony Kilner*

ABOVE The Sea Venom FAW.Mk 22 also equipped No. 893 Squadron. This unit became the first to operate this aircraft with the de Havilland Firestreak air-to-air missile although it is understood that, when this shot was made in late 1959 or early 1960, only three aircraft could carry the weapon. The picture was taken aboard HMS *Victorious* and the gentleman in the foreground is 893's Senior Pilot Lt. Cdr. Derek Matthews. *David Eagles*

Sea Venoms from No. 893 Squadron pictured in flight in 1959/60. Nearest is FAW.Mk 21 WW215 '459/V' with FAW.Mk 22 XG685 '455/V' behind. *David Eagles*

THIS PAGE Views of No. 890 Squadron Sea Vixen FAW.Mk 1s about to arrive aboard HMS *Ark Royal* in 1962. The first shows XN649 '242/R', the second XN688 '254/R'. *Richard Gravestock*

FACING PAGE TOP De Havilland Sea Vixen XJ482 '713/VL', an early production FAW.Mk 1, photographed in 1962 'armed' with dummy yellow Firestreak missiles. The aircraft was flying with No. 766 Squadron based at Yeovilton which served as the Royal Navy's All-Weather Fighter School. *David Eagles*

FACING PAGE BOTTOM Another Sea Vixen of No. 890 Squadron, XN656 '251/R', has moved into position ready for take-off from HMS *Ark Royal* in 1962. *Tony Kilner*

Sea Vixen XN708 '244/R' performs a fast and very low-level pass alongside its carrier HMS *Ark Royal* in 1963 or 1964. Considering the relative exposure speed of slide film in those days, this is a superb image. *Sir Mark Thomson*

LEFT English Electric Canberra B.Mk 15 WJ762 of No. 73 Squadron pictured over Cyprus in March 1964. *Adrian Balch*

RIGHT A mix of fighter types in RAF Germany in about 1962. Most prominent is English Electric Lightning XM179 of No. 56 Squadron (the unit markings on the nose need a repaint) taxying past Gloster Javelin XH756 to the right and Hawker Hunter XJ712 'B' of No. 14 Squadron in the background. *The late Eric Morgan*

This group of four English Electric Lightnings has aircraft drawn from different squadrons. Top to bottom – F.Mk 2 XN783 'A' of No. 92 Squadron, F.Mk 3 XP739 'H' of No. 111 Squadron, F.Mk 3 XP746 'K' from No. 56 Squadron, and F.Mk 2 XN779 'G' of No. 19 Squadron. The F.3s have the enlarged fin while the individual squadron colour schemes are very eye-catching.

ABOVE Delightful official study of Gloster Javelin FAW.Mk 7 XH756, fully armed with four Firestreaks and carrying ventral tanks, taken prior to the aircraft being fitted with Armstrong Siddeley Sapphire Sa.7R engines in 1960 in an upgrade to Mk 9 standard. *MoD*

LEFT A picture of Javelin XH886 'J' of No. 29 Squadron in 1966/67 which should bring back memories for the type's maintenance crews. The reheat jet pipes are shown to good effect.

ABOVE Although perhaps a little routine compared to some other Javelin pictures in the book, this mid-1964 view of FAW.Mk 7 XH762 'F' of No. 64 Squadron is included because its shows quite well the rather ugly in-flight refuelling probe carried by the fighter. Lightning XP696 'S' of the Air Fighting Development Squadron (AFDS) of the Central Fighter Establishment at Binbrook stands behind.

LEFT The author apologises for the smaller number of bomber photos in this album when compared to fighter types. Perhaps because of security it was not so easy for air crew to photograph the V-Bombers. Hopefully this picture will address the shortage a touch, but it is cheating a little because Handley Page Victor B.Mk 2 XH670 spent most of the 1960s performing trials with A&AEE and never joined an RAF squadron. Of course, bomber units did not decorate their aircraft in the way that fighter squadrons did, so there is nothing obvious here to suggest that this Victor is not a squadron aircraft.
Terry Panopalis

ABOVE A rare colour image showing the silver colour scheme worn by the Hawker Sea Fury aerobatic display team put up by No. 805 Squadron Royal Australian Navy in 1958. This aircraft is VX756 '100'. Note the red-painted spinner, wingtips, fin leading edge, arrestor hook and band around the cockpit canopy. *David Eagles*

FACING PAGE Pictures showing Hawker Sea Furys of Squadron VF-871 of the Royal Canadian Navy operating from the carrier HMCS *Magnificent* during the mid-1950s. *Bob Laidler via Terry Panopalis*

ABOVE Hawker Sea Hawk FB.Mk 3s of No. 738 Squadron lined up at Lossiemouth in February or March 1956. As the Naval Air Fighter School No. 738 was a part of the Operational Flying School (OFS). Nearest is WF297 '632/LM' and behind comes WF285 '630/LM'. *David Eagles*

BELOW Sea Hawk F.Mk 1 WF199 is observed being refuelled at Lossiemouth in 1956. As '699/FD' this aircraft belonged to No. 764 Squadron based at Ford. Note the yellow tail bullet. *David Eagles*

ABOVE This unusual green and white colour scheme was applied to Sea Hawk FGA. Mk 4 WV856 in early 1962 when it became an 'Admiral's Barge' in the hands of No. 781 Squadron (the Joint Officers Air Course Unit) at Lee-on-Solent. It was used by Flag Officer Air (Home) [FOA(H)] and the scheme conformed to standard naval livery but with green substituting grey on the upper surfaces. WV856 stayed with the unit until July 1967. *AE Hughes via the late Ray Sturtivant*

BELOW Pictured at Hal Far in 1960 is uncoded Sea Hawk Mk. 3 WM987 in Fleet Requirements Unit (FRU) black. When the picture was taken the aircraft had joined Hal Far's Station Flight and it was scrapped there after November 1961. Note the searchlight in the nose of the underwing pod. *AE Hughes via the late Ray Sturtivant*

The Hawker Hunter equipped a large number of RAF squadrons and the opportunity is taken here to show a few of the different markings that were applied to the type during the 1950s.

RIGHT Hunter F.Mk 4 WT802 as 'P' of No. 98 Squadron RAF Germany in 1955. This aircraft had a short life and was scrapped in 1962. *Brian Sharman via Roger Lindsay*

BELOW Hunter F.Mk 4 WV275 'D' of No. 4 Squadron RAF Germany in 1955. WV275 lasted only until June 1961 before it was broken up. *Wilfried Zucht via Gunter Kipp/Roger Lindsay*

ABOVE Another Hunter view, this time aircraft from No. 208 Squadron in 1966. This shot was included primarily to show for the modeller the sunshades above each cockpit. XE532 'K' had first flown in January 1956 as an F.Mk 6 but in 1965 was converted to FGA.Mk 9 standard.

LEFT Sapphire-powered Hunter F.Mk 5 WP183 'V' of No. 56 Squadron, photographed in about 1955. *MoD*

ABOVE AND LEFT This pair of Hunter F.Mk 6s, XE530 'A' and XF417 'B', was serving with No. 26 Squadron based at Gütersloh in West Germany when they were photographed in 1958/59. Both aircraft were eventually sold to overseas air arms. *John Merry*

LEFT Supermarine Swift FR.Mk 5s of No. 79 Squadron pictured on the flight line at Stradishall on 18 October 1959. Although based in Germany, these aircraft were visiting England for a Royal Observer Corps 'At Home' Open Day.

BELOW Wonderful view of Kai Tak at Hong Kong in 1953. In the foreground is Supermarine Spitfire PR.Mk 19 PS852 (with the tail of PS854 to the right), a Bristol Beaufighter is behind to the left and a North American Harvard trainer on the right, and the de Havilland Hornets of No. 80 Squadron stretch right across the background. The two Spitfires were detached from No. 81 Squadron at Seletar and are quite famous because from 1951 they were used on clandestine missions to photograph many important installations and airfields along the coast of Communist China. Note the concrete weights attached to PS852's wings. *Aeroplane*

After the selection of RAF Hawker Hunter views, as a balance we now have a batch showing Fleet Air Arm Supermarine Scimitar F.Mk 1 fighters.

ABOVE Scimitar XD320 '195/R' was serving with No. 807 Squadron when it was photographed in 1960 or 1961.

BELOW XD272 '102/R' belonged to No. 800 Squadron on HMS *Ark Royal* when this shot was made in 1961/62. Note the arrestor wires across the deck. In fact, these vital items in the operation of fixed wing carrier aircraft rarely make their way into a photograph.
Tony Kilner

ABOVE When pictured in the mid-1960s XD274 '114/E' was flying with No. 800B Flight aboard HMS *Eagle*. This unit was associated with but separate No. 800 Squadron with its Blackburn Buccaneers. The objective behind 800B was to build experience with in-flight refuelling – hence the beer jug logo on the fin. Note the plane guard Westland Wessex helicopter. *AE Hughes via the late Ray Sturtivant*

BELOW Scimitar XD276 pictured at the Lee-on-Solent Navy Day on 26 July 1969. This aircraft had served with No. 803 Squadron but from 1966 was used as a ground instruction airframe at Lee. *Phil Butler*

ABOVE AND LEFT Two action shots of XD268 '112/E' of 800B taken on the catapult and during launch from HMS *Eagle* in October 1964, not long after the Flight had formed. This aircraft was scrapped in 1970. *Sir Mark Thomson*

ABOVE In 1962/63 XD321 '104/R' with its distinct red fin was another Scimitar listed on the strength of No. 800 Squadron. Note the crouched attitude of the aircraft when the catapult load had been applied – and indeed some of the folk on the deck. *Tony Kilner*

LEFT Vickers Valiant B Mk 1 XD866 of No. 138 Squadron was photographed during an open day at Leconfield on 3 September 1960. The aircraft went on to serve with No. 90 Squadron before falling victim to the blanket withdrawal from service of the Valiant in 1965. *Terry Panopalis*

Index